Ireland

Ireland-ish

Written and Illustrated by

Jana Zvibleman

LUMINARE PRESS

WWW.LUMINAREPRESS.COM

Printed in the United States of America

Luminare Press
442 Charnelton St.
Eugene, OR 97401
www.luminarepress.com

LCCN: 2024913377
ISBN: 979-8-88679-638-4

*These stories are, of course, dedicated to my love,
Bruce Marbin, with whom I still travel.*

*And to my father, Leonard Zvibleman, my first,
dearest, and funniest storyteller.*

Contents

"The world is full of magic things, patiently waiting for our senses to grow sharper."

—William Butler Yeats

Toward Eire

Exportation

"What can we bring you from the United States?" we asked our soon-to-be hosts in Ireland. We figured the Irish family had acquired a few red-white-and-blue tastes when they were in the states; the American family would be missing favorite commodities from home. We made our offers not long before the last of our last-minute preparations.

Neither my husband Bruce nor I had ever traveled quite so far for quite so long, so we accepted all advice from friends, AAA, guidebooks, and travel-product catalogs. A major message: "Pack light."

I'm *not* the pack-light type. I'm the better-take-the-kitchen-sink type.

But we wanted to do this big trip right. So I exhaled and thought *minimalist*. For starters, we researched technology's latest breakthrough in underwear, manufactured of lighter-than-air microfiber, and bought a minimum number of pairs each. Measuring my shampoo-cream-rinse-other-hair-goo usage, calculating our travel days, I decided the only type of "*ugly* American" I'd be was not-perfectly-coiffed. I dribbled just what I'd need of shampoo and such, not one drop more, into little-bitty plastic travel bottles. (Well, the next day I stealthily topped the bottles off, because *ya never do know*.) Shopping in the dental-hygiene aisle, I perused toothbrushes sized for children, and wisely invested in the smallest of the tiniest bristles, fewer rows, shorter handles, to equal ever-so-many-fewer ounces.

I couldn't imagine leaving home without my dozens of scarves, essential for so many things: stylin' verve, warmth, pillowing, plus–who knows–a tourniquet? I sorted through the cotton-y, the silky, the deeply colored Indian *dupattas*, the South American rainbow weaves, the purple, the deep purple, and the bluer purple. Balancing one scarf at a time in each hand, I chose on the basis of weight only: those with the loosest weave, the thinnest fabric. Though I suffered anticipatory separation anxiety, only the two (*well, three*) very wispiest passed muster as my travel companions.

Bruce and I negotiated long and hard about deodorants, agreeing at last on one neutral-gendered, lightweight stick we were willing to share. I did stand my ground on earrings: not just one pair, but a "superfluous" pair too. Of course I chose those with the thinnest wires and teeniest ornaments.

I looked through my art supplies, necessary for self-entertainment. I could rough it: I would leave behind not one, but *several*, of the sticks of watercolor crayons. I felt quite creative and saintly, realizing I could, for instance, make double-use of the medium green and the black to *create* dark green.

I was proud of the bare-bones piles about to go into my suitcase. However, Bruce thumbs-downed my *just-in-case* pants, *what-if* additional sweaters, *emergency* socks, *can't-live-without* this and *would-really-find-comfort-in* that.

Reluctantly, I banished several supposedly non-vital items back to their drawers.

The one item that was his absolute necessity, since music was the reason for our destination: a guitar, to be coddled in its own bag. Several years before, he had entered a raffle at a music store and won a travel guitar. Its quality was nowhere near that of his valuable Martin nor his handcrafted Irish bouzouki. Yet this guitar was appropriate and also more socially acceptable than his banjos and accordion, and it was decent and sturdy, plus comparatively small, therefore perfect for this jaunt. He did include fewer little plastic picks than he wanted.

Oh, did we pack light. Each of our suitcases actually had breathing room.

So now we would be able to tuck in gifts for our hosts and hostesses. We'd be the model guests. Even though we'd tour alone before meeting up with our friends, we'd have no problem carrying around a few extra items for their pleasure. "Whatever you want!"

Then we received their lists of desires.

A pizza stone. "Pizza is *shite* here," emailed Catherine. "The very largest stone, please. The kids are growing, yeh know, and Rory's appetite, so we hafta make extra large."

Rory wanted a fishing tackle box. He fishes? A *full* kit. We found out the well-equipped box did not mean a few feathers and wires; it included pliers, knives, lures, hooks, bobbers, and sinker *weights*. One thousand million of them, all contained in a sturdy (i.e., anchor-heavy) box.

The three American children of the American family were starving for American peanut butter. Their mother would be relieved, since we asked, to get two, or three, "or more, really" of those half-gallon tubs of their favorite brand. "Chunky, please."

No, I am not making this up.

How could we refuse? So, we lugged across the ocean the heaviest treasures the New World could produce. Worth their weight in the gold at the end of the rainbow.

Irish ShmIrish

W e were about to be the rare Americans who pilgrimaged to Ireland without claiming even a smidgeon of Irish ancestry. To me, Ireland had been merely a vague, green myth. I only knew to wear green on St. Patrick's Day and to pinch those who didn't; I liked to sing "Molly Malone." Bruce, however, long felt a vital pull to the Emerald Isle. As a musician, he *noodled* his way beyond Bluegrass and for years picked and strummed traditional Celtic tunes. His love of the ol' *DI dilly DI* led us to Irish books, including *Angela's Ashes, A Star Called Henry, The Snapper,* and *The Mammy.* Plus related movies, folktales, and poetry.

Over the years, we had gotten to know several folks who hailed from Ireland. For instance Gordy, whom we met in Missouri, was born on the Emerald Isle. When he was ten, his family emigrated to Australia, where they settled into a tight Irish community. You couldn't imagine a grown man who was more of a playful lad.

The corporation Hewlett-Packard (HP) had a sister plant in Ireland, which brought to our Oregon town engineers and their families; their spunky children enlivened the Montessori school Bruce headed. Plus, the Montessori teacher training center in Ireland was a bountiful source of faculty-with-personality. Each of the Irish we encountered amused, delighted, sometimes enraged—but never bored—us. Each was such a vivid character, I became curious about what it might be like: a countryful of redheads.

Bruce just *had* to play his guitar in real Irish pubs. After years of his yearning, the stars aligned:

We became friends with the totally Irish Catherine, a classroom guide at the school, and her husband Rory, who painted the exteriors of American houses (when he wasn't painting the town red). When they moved back to their homeland, they urged us to visit. An American acquaintance was transferred to HP's Dublin plant; he and his family also invited us. Synchronistically, in the large Quaker Oats can on Bruce's dresser, our saved quarters reached the top. So we procured passports.

Thanks to our stoicism in personal packing, our luggage did, amazingly, squeak in under the airline weight limit, and *Aer Lingus Airlines* transported us overnight, literally, to that legendary land

Note: Our trip to Eire was in the olden days, 2001—that is, before the common use of cellphones, GPS, even Google. Pubs were still allowed then to be clogged with cigarette smoke, and several other particulars of the ancient land have since morphed. For these and other reasons, readers who anticipate a future visit will, fortunately or sadly, not experience a duplicate escapade.

Immersed

Navigating the *Other* English Language

We're here. Present tense. After a *looooong* flight. Our bodies know well it's really the middle of the night, yet the Irish sun's up.

We cram ourselves and our luggage into the wee rental car. Bruce takes the wheel. He considers driving to be fun. Just as important, he can't tolerate mine. He's also a confident navigator; I don't know north from, let's see, from the ceiling?

We feel we got up on the wrong side of the bed, plus all the cars are coming at us on the wrong side of the street. Each road takes us to a merry-go-round, which we will come to learn is a *ROOND-a-boot.* Bruce works on remembering to enter going left and proceed clockwise. Groggily, we perceive these traffic circles certainly do lead us in circles. Plus, this map *must* be wrong.

It's a blur, as we rush with the traffic east—*no, west*; then back west—*no, east*. For once, it's not just me who's disoriented. The traffic signs are English on the top and gobbledygook, smaller, on the bottom. Ah, we neglected to learn *Gaelic* (which is the proper name of the old, old language, yet is commonly referred to here as simply *Irish*). Bruce finally concedes, "Okay, let's ask," but we haven't seen a *petrol* station yet, so where in the world can we get directions? He pulls over by some colorful—make that *colourful*—shops. I go into the pink one and ask the proprietress how we can get to Shannon, the town which promised the establishment which promised a bed and a breakfast. All we crave, in this foreign hour, is the bed.

"Ah, yeh just head *weshhht* towards the *Jewel Carich Way*."

"Pardon me?"

"The *Jewel Carich Way*, sure, and yeh'll see it."

A man near her, leaning against the counter, nods vigorously, waving his hand in two opposite directions—Scarecrow gesturing to Dorothy on the Yellow Brick Road. "Yeah, there it will be, the Jewel Carich way."

Hmm. "Thank you."

I plunk back in the left side of the car. "We're supposed to go *weshhht*, wherever that is, to some gem place."

The Jewel Box, in my hometown of St. Louis, is a giant-sized historical greenhouse abundant with stunning plants, so I'm figuring we missed an equally special landmark. Maybe it's a display of emeralds.

West, Bruce determines, is back the way we most recently came from. All right then. His muddled brain focuses on keeping to the wacky side of the road.

Somehow through the fog around us and the fog within, we find ourselves on a highway. A divided highway. *Ah ha*, look what it says: Dual Carriageway. Get it? Why did that guy say *jewel*?

Indeed, the *way* brings our *carriage* to Shannon.

The Hurling Sons

O ur scanty research from across the world led us to
believe that residences here would all be quaint stone
cottages covered in ivy, with brightly painted shutters, and
window boxes overflowing with cheery blossoms. We arrive
in a plain residential neighborhood, all nondescript brick
boxes that could populate any older American suburb. We
find a post bearing a sign with plain block-letters, Home
Indeed, in front of the plain house bearing the address for
the Bed & Breakfast we'd reserved. All right then; the charm
of Ireland must reside elsewhere.

Jet-lagged, traffic-stunned, and language-impaired,
we're just *so* glad to be dragging our peanut-butter-tackle-
box-pizza-stone-minimalist-underwear loads up the steep
steps to the porch. We stumble to the door of our first
blessed abode in this land.

Knock knock. Within a beat, the door flings open to reveal,
we assume, the lady of the house. I'm short, yet I have a good
view of the top of her head, with tired tufts skewing hither
and yon, of that non-color to which red hair fades. On her
wizened apple-doll face, pink-framed spectacles balance
unevenly, their gold-beaded leash hanging to her bosom.
She's sporting a rumpled beige trenchcoat, which reaches
down to gray fuzzy house slippers. I identify with her dishev-
eled look, wondering whether she too has just bumped down
from an overnight flight. As we begin to introduce ourselves,
she blurts, "Ah, I thought yeh were already here."

We stand dumbly. Is this another language thing? After a
dull staring contest, she speed-mumbles, "Well-then-yeh're-
lucky-there's-the-room-ready-yeh-can-put-yer-*tings*-up-
there-top-of-the-stairs-number-three-it-is-here's-the-key-

it's-nearly-terrible-late-for-breakfast-I'll-go-wet-the-tea."

We take that as a welcome. After bumping our loads all the way up the narrow indoor staircase, which was carpeted several eras back, we find that number three is, shall we say, homey. Two low-to-the-ground twin beds sit parallel to each other, barely two hand-spans between them. They're covered by worn brown-plaid spreads which signal to me "boys." Since there's neither floor room nor closet, we heave our bags onto the beds. I lower myself also onto one, immediately figuring by its hard-lumped, uneven surface the mattress is a survivor of thousands of jumps and bangs, tickle tortures, and wrestling holds. It *is* horizontal, so it'll do. Bruce sighs, "Well, come on. Seems we're expected for breakfast." I longingly eye the magazine-thin pillow and take my leave of it.

Back downstairs, we find a small room with a rectangular table, large enough for eight, set for two. Faded, flowered cloth placemats; one napkin is pastel striped, the other neon green and covered with cartoon figures. We plunk down onto chairs whose straight backs scorn our slumped spines. A family of pale-faced redheads looks down on us from an ornate frame—molded plaster, painted gilt. There's a freckled, smiling boy squatting at his mother's knees; I could swear he's the red-haired son of our friend back home. "Look, just like Timmy McGarry when he was about ten." Then I notice the *other* boy in the picture: also Timmy McGarry, maybe twelve. Standing behind the mother and lads is balding Tim McGarry of the future.

The walls are populated up to the ceiling with photos of the two lads at every possible stage of growing up, in every possible action pose. Among the pictures hang bronze plaques, florid certificates, and blue-and-red award rosettes trailing ribbons. The world "hurling" appears here and there. The floor space is congested with end tables and shelves, breakfronts and sideboards, all bearing trophies and more sports *tchotchkes* as well as academic artifacts.

Our hostess enters, her slippers now replaced by dull-black MaryJane pumps, and she's added a cockeyed smear of pink to her lips. "I suppose yeh'd like the Irish breakfast, then."

I timidly ask, "What is the Irish breakfast, please?"

She shoots me a look that translates as "American idiot," but says, "Sausage and eggs, sausage and eggs," and turns away.

"Yes, please," Bruce calls to her back. "Uh, no thank you to the *sausage*, for both of us." We lack the energy to verify that the sausage would be pork or beef, neither of which we eat, nor do we inquire whether she has chicken or veggie alternatives. Let's keep it simple.

Over her shoulder, an even grumpier look. Lest she throw us out on the street, where we'd be far from any bed, I quickly ask, "Are those your sons then?" proud of myself to be sounding, I think, quite local.

Her face softens. "Yes, themselves indeed." Instead of following my gaze to the family portrait, she sweeps her hands around the room.

"*This* of course is the national stamp," she announces, her hand coming to rest on a framed, poster-size blow-up of an official-looking postage stamp. From it grin the two as teens in sports garb.

Ah, we realize we're sitting in a shrine to her Francis and her Brian: hurlers. Not merely hurling players, but *national* hurling *champions*. Hurling? I kinda remember skipping over a guidebook's brags about the national sport.

As if anticipating a response she's heard countless times, she says, "I *know* where you come from you thought one had to be *dead* to be on a national stamp. But here they are, the two of them!"

I'm so glad her sons, while hurling for their country, did not perish on a battlefield.

"Are they *here*?" I ask tentatively, hoping we'd plunked down our luggage in the wrong bedroom. For one thing, I'd prefer a bed large enough for us to spoon.

"Oh, *no*," she says and tells us the whereabouts of Francis and the whereabouts of Brian. I don't recognize the town or county names, but I do recognize the tone of parental pride. I also relate to the poignancy in the voice of a mother whose children are no longer frolicing on their beds upstairs, nor due to burst in the front door any minute, laughing, grimy, and smelly.

Left alone, we further contemplate the displays surrounding us, our elbows on the table, chins resting on our hands. There are Brian and Francis on the honors team, the All-Ireland. One on the "all star." Four bronzed shoes: not *baby* shoes, mind you; these are strapping-adolescent-giant athletic shoes, which obviously jogged, kicked, stomped, and pivoted, or whatever hurlers' footwear does, for many a victory before being solidified for the ages.

Our hostess eventually returns and sets in front of us ornate, chipped plates holding glumps of scrambled eggs somehow the same non-color of her hair, triangles of pale toast, and suspicious-looking reddish-pink mounds.

As I pick up a piece of toast, which is limp and lukewarm, she lingers to point out, tucked among the memorabilia, two "Certificates of Debate." Then she delicately lifts off a wall two framed Certificates of Bachelor of Arts in Business and holds them up in front of us.

It's just the two of us again, poking at the soggy and saggy mounds: tomato halves, subjected to some aggressive meddling. They look exactly the way I feel. In scurries a vertically stretched, almost-all-bald man in a pressed white dress shirt and gray suit pants, with a ruffled apron tied well above his waist. He's carrying a tray, his eyes fixed on the flowered porcelain pot, creamer, and sugar bowl, all clattering. He seems oblivious to us.

"Good morning," Bruce and I say.

No response.

"Are you the father of the hurling champions?"

"That's it!" he says brightly, now exhibiting a stiff, dentured smile as he lowers the tray onto the table. "You've seen the stamp?" he adds, rushing back through the kitchen door.

I take three sips of my first tea of this country, strong but tepid, and a few chews of the eggishness. I arrange my napkin into a loose tent over the sad tomato. We then pull ourselves back up the stairs, where we clunk down onto the twin beds formerly slept on by brother champs Francis and Brian, our first real-life-fabled Irish hurling heroes.

(We later find out from our friend Catherine that the boys' *da*, Gus Lohan our nervous waiter, was in his day also a hurling sensation.)

The Youth of Ireland

After a lumpy nap, we are ready to do Ireland. Although the beginning of our trip is designed to be on our own, we both feel eager for contact with more local folks. Spectacular and historic must-sees can come later. The hurling parents are reticent to engage about anything but their sons and eggs; they're not the hangout type. So with no itinerary, we set off wandering around Shannon, stopping in shops, pubs, wherever our fancy takes us. The sights are pleasant enough, but our anthropological urge is not satisfied by the very few, tightlipped folks we encounter for cursory exchanges of goods for money. We squish back into the car and tour aimlessly. There's Labasheeda; we read its name comes from "bed of silk," which entices us to try out this tiny village. We park and find our way by foot to a viewpoint overlooking gray stone buildings and a bay with bobbing boats. We settle in butt-worn indentations on large stones.

Suddenly, giggles, guffaws, shouts. Running across the scene below, a passel of teens, carrying plastic bottles and buckets and jugs, shoving against the side of a building, bumping each other at an outside faucet, filling their vessels, and heaving water: boys at the girls/girls at the boys/boys at the girls. I mean, lasses and lads. The lasses wear gray-and-blue- plaid school-uniform skirts, knee-high socks, cardigan sweaters. The lads are in dark blue pants, white shirts. We're riveted.

A caterwaul of
"NYAHH-HA!" splashes "EEEIIIIIIIIYYY!" run run away, cower and scream
"I NEED A REFILL!" swoop to the faucet "EEEEK!" cluster

and cling and break away "REFILL!" "ME FIRST" "GOT YA" "ARRGGH!" scramble and push "REFILL!" "ARGGHHHH!" tumble, dive "FIVE-MINUTE BREAK!" "NO, NO BREAK!" "EEEEK!" "AAAK!" "REFILL!" "HA!!" "SAFETY!"

Each of them, ecstatic and miserable, flings half an ocean at the others. Suddenly, a blast that could shake any deaf or dead:

"LADS! I'M WRUNG!"

It's from the wide mouth of a tall, black-haired, heavily freckled lass, dripping head to toe.

What a great introduction to the regional spirit! We haven't interacted, yet we're safer this way, observing the adolescents of the indigenous species from a distant perch.

Rollin'

Despite our general disorientation, sitting in a car next to Bruce is grounding for me. While he works at driving, I gaze at his profile: he's as handsome as when we met thirty years ago. When I had first brought him to my family's home, Aunt Mollie whispered to me, "He has a beautiful nose, but what does he *look* like under that beard?" Now, his chin and cheeks are clean-shaven, yet he's retained his mustache. It and his abundant head curls are dark chocolate. My Aunt Lucille, a hairdresser, squeals every time she sees him, "The ladies in my shop would kill for those curls!" Framing his hazel-ish eyes, his glasses are John-Lennon round. It's always easy for me to sketch his likeness—all you need are those curls, mustache, and glasses, plus the so-called beauty mark on his right cheek.

From the first time I heard his singing voice, it has touched me, though his musical standards are higher than mine, and he's modest about his own sound. With my ignorance about music, I can describe his voice only as male, tenor, and corduroy-soft. Over the years, hearing him sing, I often exclaim, "I just fell in love with you again!"

He grew up in Philly snapping his fingers to groups of groovy Black teens harmonizing on street corners. In contrast, the live music of my childhood was the likes of "Old MacDonald" in school, and my Dad belting out *la-dee-da-dee-da* when driving; the grooviest album in our home was *The Sound of Music*. I eventually made it to Pete Seeger; Peter, Paul and Mary; Judy Collins. Ed Sullivan brought the Beatles into my living room, but I didn't pay them much attention. Then in college a friend gave me

Cheap Thrills with Janis Joplin.

Past my teens, when Bruce and I got together, I was amazed at how he'd hear the first three notes (or chords?) of any contemporary music and name the piece plus the band. He owned piles of LPs, including blues, old-timey, and blue grass.

He brought me more up-to-speed on our generation's music via his records, a few concerts, and the car radio. Now on our frequent road trips, we sing. Our typical set: I start us on, "And you know that you can trust her/ for she's touched your perfect body with her mind." He leads in, "Big wheel keep on turning/ Proud Mary keep on burning." We do, "Your flag decal won't get you into heaven anymore" and "Hey Jude." He teaches me, "I met her one day in a candy store/ She turned around and smiled at me/ Get the picture?"

I remember lyrics; it's Bruce who is in tune and on key and knows how to harmonize.

At work in the Montessori classroom, we sing the top tens of the three-to-six-years-olds, such as "I Am a Pizza," plus Bruce's originals that teach the parts of trees, mushrooms, flowers.

But this trip is for *Irish* music. Though his fingers itch to pluck his hundreds of tunes, in transit we share a small repertoire of songs. We shun the sappy "Danny Boy," yet Bruce is elated by dorky ditties such as "Who put the overalls in Mrs. Murphy's chowder?" and "Bobby's britches gone off in the tide/ What is he going to do, oh?" We both like, "I am bound to leave my Nancy/May I go along with you?/ Oh no, my love! Farewell," a sad romance which is Celtic if not specifically Irish.

Eire on the Air, or, The Death Has Occurred

I t's not long before Bruce manages to work the car radio dial past the modern Irish rock noise to *Clare FM*, the traditional (*trad*) radio station, so now during every ride we tune in to the *DI dilly DI*. It sounds identical to what he listens to and plays in America at jams, practices, and performances. Now he calls out every title: "Whisky in a Jar"; "Hanagan's Hooley"; "Song for Ireland." Whatever.

Between the jigs and reels and an occasional *a cappella* air comes the news. Or is it sports, or is it political commentary, or humor? We have no clue, as the male voice is not speaking English. We applaud the effort to reclaim and revive the mother tongue, which was squashed by, who else, England. Now, by national mandate, children learn Irish in school. As I noted, every traffic sign bears English, in Roman type, as well as Irish, in script which fascinates us, its stout shapes peppered by accents and dots, pronounced *who-knows-how*. Now hearing the language spoken as it should be, we construe it as a mixture of Yiddish and Hebrew, with bonus German-ish throat events.

Yet periodically we *can* understand what is being said. Why in the world is *English* the language of the Death Notices?

Thus our deepest cultural immersion to-date is with the dead of County Clare. Either throngs of people drop on the half-hour throughout every day, or Clare FM offers each notice redundantly so the bereaved are sure to catch his/her loved one's parting fame. Or, maybe the station spreads out the bad news so as not to overwhelm the listener with the daily deceased in one fell swoop. In any case, in our short stay in this country, we are privy to a wealth of Death Notices. The deep male voice intones somberly, yet at a rapid clip with no pauses, presumably to avoid dead (*sorry*) airtime: "The death has occurred of Cormac O'Mahon, Ballyduneen, Knockalough and late of Barefield. Human removal this Wednesday evening to Glasneven Crematory. All friends and neighbors welcome. The death has occurred of Kathleen Keirnan, 64 McClare Villas. Respects this evening at the home. The death has occurred of Queeva. . .." *Queeva?*

The grand finale of each list is the obligatory "May they rest in peace," efficiently covering the lot of Clare's newly late.

Indulge

We're in Galway, on Shop Street. One teal-colored entryway seems a magnet for men, women, and children. Quaint gold letters identify Griffin's. Now, I'm normally not one to jump on a bandwagon, but I sense these folks are *onto* something. I shoulder into the wide, bulgy queue, all bodies aiming toward the door, jumbling at a glacial pace closer to it and each other. Shuffled along, I identify the sirens' call: a warm, sugary, spicy aroma. Now I see a highly polished plaque which brags about the exemplary delicacies offered at this establishment and about the award granted to the proprietors in the late 1800s. Ultimately in the doorway, I stand on my toes and contort, straining to see above, around, and below heads and shoulders. A glass case displays white cakes and brown cakes, cookies, scones, muffins, shortbreads, pies, and tortes. Each seems the most desirable on earth, until my gaze rests on the next. I read labels: grinder, cottage loaf, Bailey's cheesecake. How will I choose, *if* I ever get a turn? Millimeter by millimeter, closer, closer. Now, a thicket of humanity is behind me, with but one man and woman in front. They're discussing the cheesy fruity crumbly hunk of heaven held up at an angle by a lady in white behind the counter. The couple is gravely debating with each other: they don't *need* all that, do they, for very good reasons, you know, but would it be a mistake to order only the two, no four slices they *should* indulge in, because, as the bakery lady instructs, the whole of it becomes a *splendid buy,* well, perhaps just this once, for the sake of the pocketbook, although . . ..

Okay already. Grabbing the opportunity to put my fellow humans out of their misery, as well as to nab a treat at bulk price, I shout, "Take the lot of it! I'll pay you for whatever portion you don't need."

I'm thankful they comprehend my language; the deal is struck. I cross their palms with silver and, cradling my treasure, squeeze out through the lusting horde. Bruce is across the street listening to the music of buskers, his fingers twitching on imaginary frets. "We have to sit down immediately," I insist. "Here, on the curb."

This sugary manna is perfection in our mouths, and we understand why man-and-womankind has salivated in front of Griffin's Bakery for a goodly chunk of history.

Redheads

Now we're on a bus. I whisper to Bruce, "Turn around, over there—that redhead. Not *that* one, that one *behind* him. The spitting image of Amelia, right?"

Red hair is as common here as are stories. At home, I could count on one hand the redheads I've known: there was that skinny, rowdy boy across the street from my childhood home. Carla-the-Bully in my grade school. The aforementioned Tim and Gordy. Adorable Amelia.

Okay, on *two* hands. Our friends in Massachusetts, black- and brown-haired themselves, have a daughter born with the hair of Pippi Longstockings. By age three, Elena disliked the attention brought on by her stand-out locks. Whenever a stranger would begin, "Wow, what a beautiful head of . . . ," she flew into a rage. Of course, by shrieking and stomping off, she thereby fueled the stereotype about the redheaded temperament. Elena's parents should relocate her to Ireland, I now realize. Rather than suffering endearments such as "carrot top," she would enjoy full camouflage.

Also, my dear Jane McVeigh, whose mother was a Peg and father a Joe. Jane still lives in close proximity to a typically abundant Irish-American passel of sisters, cousins and nieces, brothers and grandnephews.

I do research. Red hair, accompanied by pale skin and freckles, is due to a mutated gene that fails to produce sun-protective, skin-darkening "eumelanin." As ancients with that gene migrated from central Asia to Northern Europe, they could thrive because their pale skin produced vitamin D efficiently in the wan sunlight. One advantage of their thus-strengthened bones: the women were better equipped to survive pregnancy and childbirth.

As little Elena must have sensed, descriptors including red, carrot-topped, ginger, strawberry blond, auburn, and chestnut locks are each tangled through with connotations and judgements. These have varied according to gender and status. Mark Twain, whose ancestry included Scots-Irish, wrote, "When red-headed people are above a certain social grade their hair is auburn." And also, "You know I like color and flummery and all such things—I was born red-headed—maybe that accounts for my passion for the gorgeous and ornamental."

(No matter what your hair color, whisper the word "flummery," and I'll follow you anywhere.)

For my first few days in Ireland, I think, "They all look alike." In my defense, I believe that's a classic perspective of almost any outsider to almost any culture. Further, I'll bet that to space aliens, all earthlings—of any hair and skin pigmentation, nose shape, height—look alike.

And so, just as with the hurling brothers, I continue to mistake people here for one of "our" redheads. "There *is* Tim McGarry! I swear. See him? On the bridge, that young guy carrying the huge bass fiddle. It's more than his hair, it's his face and body too. Yeah, I *know* Tim doesn't play bass. Maybe he's here in Ireland visiting his father's long-lost clan. Or, that's his identical third cousin."

The Children of Lir

"Oh, look: swans!"

I'm no virgin to swan-sightings. I've gawked at not one but two pairs of long-necked beauties in the pond in Ashland, Oregon, decorating that Shakespeare Festival town. But never have I imagined so many swans together as here by Galway Bay. Eighty, or a hundred, or two hundred? A swan swarm. Actually, Professor Guidebook calls it a *bank* of swans.

We settle onto a bench *just for a few minutes* to admire them. They invite us to get out our sketchbooks; an hour later, I am on my umpteenth attempt to capture *essence d' swan* with black ink, and red and orange watercolor crayons, on white paper.

They're floating, squatting, nipping, ruffling, three or four yards away. I creep closer to take a gander, so-to-speak. (Sorry. The male swan is the *cob*.) Though I don't sense a "Howdy, Jana, welcome to our waters," they tolerate me. They are much too busy preening, definitely focused on maintaining appearances. Even though I'm uncamouflaged, this is not a fleeing flock.

If they *were* to take flight, in the air they'd be a *wedge*.

I squat on the pebbles at the water's edge, face-to-beak with them. Ah, such poetic beings. Symbols of love, fidelity, tranquility.

Well, close up, these guys are not eye-candy; the ugly duckling might have ended up better as some other species. Their reputation for grace must have been promoted by near-sighted viewers from a distance. Swan bodies are thick, their plumage dingy. At the top of each beak, kind of between the eyes, is a tumorous-looking bumpy lump;

if that's meant to be a *pleasing* feature, it's so only to other swans. (On the males, I later learn, it swells during the breeding season. Ick.) The gawky, awkward poses as they contort their necks, reaching, pecking at their own skin: not a ballet. Nor are their squawks ethereal.

Wanting to appreciate these guys, I do make one discovery that could count as aesthetically pleasing: at *very* close range, I can see through the two holes in their beaks! Not to their innards, but right through: the nostrils, I guess they are, frame the blue sky above the bay. Rather picturesque.

Considerable swan debris gooks up the ground; the only items of interest to me are the moltings. I select feathers greedily: free souvenirs. The largest is long, thick, stiff, intact—quite the find. A pinion? From a wing? I'll whittle the end to a point and dip the quill in handground ink to pen my opus, I will.

Then, with reluctant reality, I toss it back down in the muck; while it's a romantic idea, ballpoints and keyboards make composing much easier. That was just a dirty castoff; I must stay mindful of my suitcase's heft. Yet, I do pocket three weightless, white fluffs. Maybe I'll start a down mattress.

Leaving the swan party, I return to Bruce at our bench, hoping to regain an appreciation of the birds' beauty.

After a beat, I blurt out, "I wonder why people don't *eat* swans."

I'm regarding their chests: exaggeratedly ample bosoms. There's meat there. Isn't this a practical country? What about the potato famine? These people make use of the very *turf* for fuel; why would they allow main dishes to glide idly by? (Ah, because *glide idly by* sounds like *DI dilly DI*? Okay, I reign in my poet-brain.) Might thigh-of-swan be a hidden ingredient in the infamous Irish stew?

We pack up our paints, leave the bench, and stroll back towards the footbridge. With distance, the swans do regain elegance.

Looking down from the bridge, I notice an old man in classic-looking work get-up, from cable knit cap to heavy-duty black bib overalls to sturdy boots. He's balancing in a wobbly little tied-up sailboat, coiling ropes and fastening metal gadgets.

"Hello!" Bruce and I call.

(Catherine's 90-year-old aunt had criticized her for coming home from America with the habit of "Hi." "*Hi* is not a proper greeting," the aunt admonished. "'Tis only *half* a greeting." So while on this turf, we're mindful of Hellos.)

The boat-guy looks up and waves; we exchange pleasantries. Then I ask, "Excuse me, but why don't people eat swans?"

He pauses in his work and gazes at me.

"Well, ya know," he says, leaning towards us, speaking slowly, "They don't taste good. They don't taste good at all!"

He turns away, proceeding to fiddle with traps and waders and lures, or whatever they are. Then, he looks back over his shoulder at us. "Besides, there *are* the *legends!*"

Later, among Lester's picture books, we happen upon "The Children of Lir." As it goes, a beloved mother died, leaving four *weans*. Their father Lir remarried; of course, true to the misogyny of patriarchal literature, the stepmother was a rotten apple. To rid herself of those brats, she contracted with a witch. This one didn't have an appetite for boys and girls, apparently, as in classic tales we grew up with. Instead of gobbling them up, the hired sorceress turned them into swans. The sibling swans suffered years of the harshest storms and most treacherous seas, in wretched places. I'm guessing an authentic Irish storyteller, *a seanchaí* (pronounced *SHAN uh kee*), would elaborate with details horrific enough to make a child's knickers quiver, but Lester's book is somewhat PG13. Despite it all, these children/swans survived and stayed together. By and by, through some fateful intervention, they were transformed back into humans. Yet to this day, it is said, any swan just *might* be one of the Children of Lir. And so, of course, there's no harming a swan.

In bed that night, Bruce and I discuss the fable. Abandoned children, we know, is a common theme in folktales, "Hansel and Gretel" *et al*, probably because of a common childhood fear. We each understand it. Neither of us as children lost a parent to death, but Bruce was abandoned by his father, a rogue. I, as a young child, was clingy; when left in the strange world of kindergarten, I was inconsolable. Also, I grew up knowing that my maternal grandma's mama died during her birth. Her father quickly remarried a woman found by a matchmaker; his new wife turned out to be the stereotypical cruel-stepmother. We go to sleep heartened that those Lir waifs managed.

Yet I ponder, how did the boat man *know* swans don't taste good?

One Small Town

Ennistymon, it says. The town's not made it into our guidebooks. Looks drab, drippy. Nevertheless, we both need to stretch, so in Ennistymon we stop. It's easy to find a place to park; the whole populace must be out to lunch in Paris. Silence. We wander by foot through the drizzle, looking into windows for indications of life. A shuttered storefront. Locked-up book shop. Locked-up music shop, where Bruce lingers to peer in at the darkened display of guitars and fiddles. I start across the street and am stepping around potholes when I hear a deep voice, "Are you French?"

I look up. Three feet in front of me, on the other side of a pit that could hold a dead Irish Wolfhound, is a black-haired, ruddy-faced man. He's big in every dimension, scraggly in every inch. I guess his age to be mid-forties.

He sounds oddly both gruff and gentle. "Uh, French, or *American* are you?" What gives me away as an invader even before I open my mouth?

Bruce appears next to me, takes my hand, and we identify our origin. The man claims his home as New Zealand.

"This is a *boring* town," he volunteers. "One *tousand* people. Nothing interesting at all in this town. Only the cascade, the only *ting* here. Go down there and walk over the bridge and back that way, it's very nice, the river and the falls, the only *ting* worth it here."

He continues without prompting, "I'm living here now, well, I'm *stuck* here, I don't have the means to go elsewhere. I'm looking for work. This is a terrible town.

"I'd like to go home, I would. But here I am."

I've learned an Irish word for his state of mind: *begrudgery*. Makes me think of how my Jewish culture shares that world view, for sad historical reasons. In Yiddish, this habitual complainer would be a *kvetch*.

"Well then," I offer, myself in an upbeat mood, "I'll *see*, umm, *imagine* you arriving *home*."

He tilts his head, raises his thick, dark eyebrows, stares quizzically at me.

Breaking the silence, we all bid goodbyes and good-lucks, and Bruce and I stroll off in the direction he pointed. We *go down there and walk over the bridge and back that way*.

A narrow street takes us to a sign: The River Inagh. A low, skinny waterfall, anemic, as waterfalls go. Here I make good on my *woo-woo* declaration: I visualize our homesick acquaintance leaning against the railing of a ship being pushed by strong winds away from Ireland. I picture him brightening at the sight of his homeland, leaping down the gangway, and kneeling, kissing his New Zealand soil. Now he's reaching his arms up, hugging his very own sky. I imagine him flashing back to the strange American woman in the street in that terrible trap, Ennistymon. And for a moment his smile holds a wondering: Could it be? Could the odd thing she said have anything to do with this blessed homecoming?

And I say it did.

I leave my vision bubbling in the water below, and we retrace our steps through the quiet lanes. Gradually, I'm moping along. Oh, how classic and how sad. A place where a person gets stuck. Yes, what a dismal town; you can see that he's right. It's wan, worn, devoid of animation. The very stones of the buildings here are weary. No colors. Even the weeds don't flower. The air itself is gray, gray.

I remember the stomachache of homesickness. Sixth-grade camp, my first time far from parents, was a glorious adventure with my best friend. *Except* for the third afternoon, when I cried and cried against our counselor's shoulder. Years later, finding myself away within an immense university, I physically and emotionally "freaked out." Now I contemplate how I've never been homesick when traveling with Bruce. He is my home.

Turning a corner towards our car, we suddenly hear musical chatter: the lilt of children's voices, eager sounds. They're calling to us.

"Take our picture!"

"Will yeh take our picture?"

"One of *all* of us!"

"An' one of *me*." "An' of *me*!" "An' of *me*!" "An' one of *me*!"

Four girls of varying heights are now beside us, bouncing on the footpath. Three are redhead; one is chubby and tall; one is dark; two are tiny, skinny. There are freckles, ponytails, pigtails, skirts. All are smiling, jumbled in a clump with two bikes.

"Sure," Bruce says, readying the camera.

"In exchange," I interject, "I'd like you to tell us: what do you like about your town?"

"The swimming pool! The swimming pool!" they all exclaim, pointing up the hill to the old stone building on the corner, labeled *Community Centre*.

"There's a pool," one says. "And *snooker*," says another, dragging out that *oo* as they do with *pool*.

For a silent split second, they hold still and smile sweetly, toothily, toward the camera. Then they resume moving in a clot alongside us, pushing and pulling their bikes, blumbering and bobbing along, answering more potential questions than even *I* could ask.

"My name's Erica an' she's my sister." "An' we're sisters

an' she's my cousin an' she's my cousin an' she's *her* sister."

"We're Conners but they're Flanders, we're all Byrnes."

"Doreen." "Jane." "Mairead."

"I have a sister named Onagh an' one named Mary an' another named Stephanie an' another named Fiona."

"An' I have a brother named Aidian an' one named Patrick and Conner an' . . ."

"I have seven sisters and three brothers!" "I have five brothers an' two sisters."

"An' I'm going to New York!" "An' I'm going to England!"

When we stop at our car and open the doors, the girls collide with each other just short of jumping in with us. We all laugh and wave, call goodbyes, wave more. As we pull away, I feel in my bones what a lovely town is Ennistymon, and what a grand day to be in it.

The Craggy

We've stopped in Doolin and popped into a turquoise-painted shop to phone the host of our next B&B for directions.

"Ah, yer already in the town a' Doolin, are yeh? Then you'll find the Craggy Island Bed and Breakfast a fifteen-minute drive from where yeh stand."

So we get back in the car and proceed past two other shops, a hostel, four pubs, and a café. I scratch my nose and Doolin is gone. We drive up a long, gradual hill, nothing but farmland, farmland, and farmland. The road turns into a *boreen*: a lane narrow as Bruce's guitar's neck, with high weeds whiskering the middle ridge between muddy ruts.

I'm chanting my new mantra: "Drive on the left side. Drive on the left side." Bruce doesn't even consider it nagging. Yet there is no left side. This one-lane path must have been made for a horse. A skinny horse. We're squeezed mere centimeters (however long a centimeter is) from the dark green hedgerows to our right and left. I recognize their pinky-purple blossoms as fuschia, though these are the size of my fist, while their American counterparts are smaller than my pinky. And *our* fuchsias hang tamely from pots; here they stand wild and tall as the giant Finn McCool (which is the coolest name, isn't it?). It's as if we're in a tunnel, with no peripheral views—a shame, since our mission as tourists is to view everything. I roll down my window, hoping to breathe in fragrance.

Though the course is straight as an Irish dancer's arms, Bruce has to concentrate on driving, especially managing the shift stick with his left hand. I'm in fear the branches might—should the car tilt sideways at the inevitable next pothole—scrape my face. But I keep the window open, maybe so I can call for help. I stifle my squeals and, as self-therapy, shut my eyes. Which makes it trickier to be of any help in looking for the turn-off.

I peek—I gasp: a humongous truck is approaching. No space here to *do-si-do*; this is beyond even Bruce's masterful driving skills. *Oh Brigid, we could use some protection here. Or whichever Celtic goddess/saint: Come in please. Maybe Maeve — isn't she the patron of travelers? Yeah, we're Jewish, but hey, shouldn't miracles be nondenominational?*

Had I the presence of mind to call up the expression, I might declare we are *on tenterhooks*. For now, I'm simply scared to death.

Minutes or a second later, the truck driver/farmer so kindly pulls over a good three inches, which accommodates our vehicle, inscrutably. *Thank you, good job, ye Patronesses.*

Taking the luxury of breaths again, we continue on. Ah, there's a house. I get up the gumption to knock on the door. Through a window I see a child bouncing by. The door opens to a man without a shirt. To my apologies and query, he says, "Well then, Craggy Island, is it? Let me see, ah yes, well, I don't know. Did you come from Lisdoonvarna on the road?"

It's fun to recognize that name from one of Bruce's standard tunes, "The Road to Lisdoonvarna," but no, we haven't been there.

"Oh, no, well then this road here you must have come on. That road, well, if you go down—oh, that's where you came, is it? Well, it's down there, there'll be the sign Craggy Island, you see, that blue house? Well, you'll pass it, not this crossroad but go to the next, pass over that crossroad then when you come to another, and then you'll see it, it's off down to the left, a house, yes."

To my thanks, he says, "That's okay. I didn't hear the door, we use the other one you see, so I didn't know what it was. Oh fine, that's all right yes, g'day."

Twenty, thirty minutes and countless jolts later, a crossroads. Here are arrows pointing to an array of choices, of an array of lovely towns with an array of lovely names, in two languages. But no sign of the sign for *Craggy Island*. Nor *any* B&B.

Without phone booth, nor *star to steer her by*, it seems wise to turn back towards now-distant Doolin. Maybe one of its pubs has an upstairs room to let? A place called *craggy* may not be much of a haven anyway.

With sighs, we retreat via the ruts to whence we came.

Eventually—a long-in-coming eventually—look, look! The sweet word: **Craggy**.

Aha, we *get* it. That gracious truck was at the exact spot, and was just high enough, to obscure this marker and this turn-off.

I'd hug Bruce for joy, if such maneuvers were possible in this cramped car. I also want to get out and dance a proverbial jig. Except that would take up time, and we'd rather gun it.

So onto the gouged sideroad we go, and after only a few more clonks and clatters, we thunk to a stop in front of a house—a *gaff*. A bright-white *gaff*. It stands solo in the midst of grassy field, field, and field, with behind it a field. Through its windows, warm, golden light glows a welcome.

The Craggy makes all our travel travails worthwhile. Before we reach the door, a man with soft eyes and a sweet smile is greeting us. Nothing craggy about him: his face is smooth, his expression soft. He's maybe in his forties. His hair is not red but light brown, curly. It feels natural to share hugs with him, as if we've reunited with a fond cousin. Inside, the aroma is of fresh-baked bread, with an undertone of roses; the light-gold couches and chairs look cushy. This is also a personal art gallery: each richly colored wall, maroon, brown, forest green, displays landscape paintings that invite us into woodlands and seas. An oval frames the Irish blessing, "May the holes in your nets be no larger than the fish in it." A side table holds a colored-pencil drawing of a man who resembles our host himself, younger, cradling a guitar.

He prepares the best-tasting tea we've had in this land. A lidded container holds what he explains is coarse beet sugar, the typical sweetener here. Along with warm soda-drop biscuits, he also serves us enthralling insider stories about the local culture, nearby outings, and his B&B life.

"You're a musician?" I say. "That's you with the guitar in the drawing?"

Yes he plays; mostly he sings. "I used to travel with it, the music," he says. "But now it's occasionally only, and only at a pub in town."

We feel refreshed as we climb the stairs to our room, which features a homemade pastel patchwork quilt and a vase of fresh flowers. A white long-haired cat appears at the open window and jumps right in for a lingering purr.

In the morning, breakfast is generous and delicious. When we made the reservation, this host inquired about our dietary preferences, and look, he heeded them: he's cooked up Linda McCartney Brand sausage—who knew Linda is vegetarian? Oh, and his toast is, surprise, toasty.

In the day we brave the hazards of the road to drive back to Doolin. We experience the Cliffs of Moher, try out pub grub (nothing to write home about, yet the *taytos* are salty and greasy enough to satisfy). We people-watch to our hearts' content, and Bruce plucks enough *DI dilly DI* to make proud our friend Quaker on our emptied oats can.

We had booked two nights here. Let's treat ourselves to a Craggy bonus night; our host is happy to accommodate. He seems so content blending his life and his work, making it look so easy, I contemplate hanging up a B&B shingle when we return home.

Because he's a musician, every day we anticipate hearing him sing and strum. No such sounds. So, during our final Craggy breakfast, I dare, "Maybe, before we take off, Bruce could play along with you? Would you sing us a song or two?"

"No," he shoots back, uncharacteristically abrupt. "I won't play music this week."

"Oh." I wonder whether a punchline is coming. Or perhaps it's custom that, for humility's sake, the Irish require cajoling to display their talents. (Hmm, that was the way of Chinese people we've known, but does it ring true with the Irish?)

Long pause. He's been gazing out the window but now glances back at our looks of puzzlement. "I won't play," he repeats. "My mother died a week ago, in England actually. So I won't be playing music this week."

There's been no hint, in his pleasant and relaxed manner, of this grief in his heart. Holding back exclamations of surprise, we offer our condolences.

I contemplate the downside of the B&B business. He's had to keep his very home open to strangers, during what my parents would call *a time like this.*

"Yes, well the funeral's coming up," he continues. "A

week it has been."

"Will you go there?"

"What? Will I *go there*? Oh, I'd tread over heaven and earth to get there. Yes, *of course* I will go!"

I had packed print-outs of several of my poems, optimistic I might find an opportunity to share them. This may be it. I'm emboldened because I've read that in the "old days" in rural Ireland, people were hungry for fun and distraction, so whenever a stranger arrived, they'd be asked, "What do yeh have to entertain us with?"

So when we go back up to our room to gather our things and pet farewell to the cat, I re-open my suitcase, push around shirts and socks, find my folder, and rifle through loose pages searching for a poem about the passing of my own mother. Dang, seems I didn't include it in my traveling collection. So I select another that may give balm:

> *To my (winter) self*
>
> now   I write to you   while the window   is still open
> letting breezes in, light   remember
> now   I write to you   to say   you're not alone
> numbed   in this room   reaching   for a sweater
>
> I visit you,   sit   where you sit,   drink tea together
> (brewed of peppermint, raspberry   leaves
>   that I gather now
>   that I dry now
>   that are growing now   in the sun)
>
> I'm with you,   preserving aroma   so you won't be
>   without,   or forget

Look   on this table   peaches   plums   grapes
fruit   and flowers   I save for you   I bring to you
dried   to their ageless colors

you'll see   me   here   take this picture
by the window   with you   now
and around the table   together
you'll return   with me

meanwhile   hold   warmth   in your cup
keep   the fire

Well, to me it's a poem of comfort and hope; who knows
what he'll think.

After we settle the bill and pack the car, I hand the folded
paper to our bereaved host, saying he might want to read
it later, it's just a small thing I have to offer for his troubles.

Moher and More

We were told by guidebooks and natives to prepare for *breathtaking* and *majestic*. The Cliffs of Moher *are* all that. Yet we noticed no warning of the trudge up on infinite, rugged stone steps. We jostle among other foreign pilgrims, elbow-to-hip-to-head-to-knee, all bearing binoculars, cameras, bottles, sandwiches, all stopping here and here for *one more* photo. We read of the beauty to be seen here "on a clear day." Thank you very much; it's clear *this* day is only gray on gray. For gray, we could have stayed in Western Oregon.

Along comes a wind almost strong enough to blow us all against the cliff wall—or with a change of course, off it. Now a downpour, which gets most of the tourists yelling, in English, French, German, "Why the hell didn't *you* bring an umbrella?" No, I don't speak French or German, but *ya know* what they're saying. Others are wailing, in the Babel of languages—again, trust me—"Damn, my new binoculars will be ruined!" A lone Irish voice chuckles, "Just a rain squall, this."

We struggle with the crowd toward the highest point on the cliffs and possible refuge: **O'Brien's Tower**. Ooh, this could be noteworthy—perhaps a storied sanctum for royalty. Guess not: the plaque says it was built in 1835 and served as a common teahouse. Ah, a hot *cuppa* would be splendid. We duck in through the doorway.

Right. Up on this grand natural landmark, with a supposedly breathtaking view, we find ourselves in a small room cluttered with price tags. This commercial establishment offers green leprechaun trinkets and green horoscope bookmarks. Green packets of "Authentic Irish Incense" (which, we guess, recreates the ambient aroma in this room: dank and musty). We exit back to the weather and huddle against the stone wall to do what we know well how to do: watch rain.

A man leaning against the same wall, enhancing the atmosphere with his cigarette's gray emissions, informs us in indignant tones that his radio told him it's a clear, blue sky, sunny day at home in England. He proceeds to broadcast his gripes about "this pissing Irish weather," when he could be "across the water sitting on my arse back home," and he wonders "why the fuck anyone would squander breath in this G-d-forsaken country."

Bruce and I shuffle away to the railing.

I search through foggy binoculars. For a moment, there's a view, and I can make out squillions of seabirds, though I wouldn't know a puffin from a kittiwake, razorbill, or guillemot; maybe they're all gulls. Anyway, it's awesome, the multi-lingual chatter of both the birds and the humans around me, who point at and praise the majestic white splotches on the cliffs: droppings.

The opaque gray curtain lowers again. I know I am facing towards mountains, island, yet all merge together; barely an outline.

My eyes become moist, but not from the mist. I don't know why this soft, amorphous oneness—landscape, seascape, and skyscape—moves me to tears. I sense I'm sharing a sacred vision. This must be the true magnificence hovering between the lines of the guidebooks. Eire, you've softly touched me. Though I've heard your songs over and over (and over) in folk-music circles, I only now truly feel the sentiment. I can now comprehend why the laments are crooned and passed down by your daughters and sons, who left you of harsh necessity for distant shores, yet keep gazing back.

Jig of Slurs

W e had picked up the term *DI dilly DI* from one of the first Irish people we knew, Mairead Connoly, a Montessori teacher in Oregon. When Bruce tried to celebrate Celtic music with her, she confided, "I can't stand that old *DI dilly DI*."

Mairead's lack of enthusiasm for that part of her heritage could not dampen Bruce's loyalty for a music *his* ancestors never knew from. For twenty years, he has picked, noodled, and strummed, and for twenty years I've been groupie, roadie, and audience for plucking practice, jam sessions, and performances. I *can* stand *DI dilly DI* (yet not for *all* of the ten thousand hours Bruce is determined to log). According to the musicians, they play hundreds of different reels, jigs, slip-jigs, airs, polkas, slides, and waltzes, with a planxty tossed in here and there. According to me, they're all the same.

The extent of the musical savvy I've gained from Bruce: a tune is different from a song. The former is instrumental, the latter has lyrics.

As a poet, I find true value in the evocative titles in his current band's repertoire: "Tripping Up the Stairs" "Banish Misfortune "Drowsy Maggie" "Wind That Shakes the Barley" "Jig of Slurs" "The Star Above the Garter" "Saucy Sailor" "Adieu Sweet Lovely Nancy" "Connaughtman's Rambles" "Star of the County Down" "Merrily Kiss the Quaker's Wife" "Down by the Sally Gardens" "When I Go" "Angeline the Baker" "Money in Both Pockets" "Possum Up a Gum Stump." Plus "O'Carolan's Farewell to Music" and dozens of other O'Carolan's this's and O'Carolan's thats.

Should I ever have the opportunity to christen a tune, I'm thinking, "O'Carolan's Hiccups." Or, autobiographically,

"Vomiting Green Beer at 18" and "Zvibleman the Band Roadie." I long ago lobbied Bruce to compose "Jana's Scarves"; I'm still waiting. He did compose "Green Eyes"—no words to it, but I know that's his "Here's lookin at you, kid" to me. Another of his originals is "Pass the Fez," referring to the classic Turkish cap shaped like the frustum of a cone, made of felt, with a tassel. His tune commemorates a *leopard-skin* fez which made the rounds from head-to-head at a Halloween party and ended up in Bruce's side of our closet.

Pub Talk

A t pub after pub, Bruce does achieve his dream of joining in *sessions*. It's not that he claims a speck of appropriate blood. Coursing through his veins *are* Celtic F sharps, Gs, octaves, jigs, and tunes. They trill out through his fingers into the strings of his guitar and Irish bouzouki (bizz *OO* kee), also called mando-cello—like an oversized mandolin.

Anyway, his soul resonates with Celtic music, and at last we've gotten him to the mother lode, where he heads straight into every public house that has a hand-scrawled announcement in the window, Session Tonight. Most pubs do. At these open-to-all music jams, men and women circle up on straight-backed wooden chairs and pull out flutes, fiddles, banjos, hammered dulcimers, harps, guitars, penny whistles, Irish bouzoukis, mandolins. Also, uilleann (*ILL ee un or ILL un)* pipes, an Irish bagpipe pumped with the elbow. And bodhràns (*BOW rawn*), a shallow drum held sideways and struck with a two-headed drumstick.

The musicians seem to joyfully and easily blend together into their common art, even with newcomers among them. As Bruce's fanclub, I've long been fascinated with how making music is called *playing*. I envy that spirit. In my chosen creative pursuits, we're not called *players*. It's rare to find a visual artist, much less a writer, who "plays well with others."

Bruce orders a pint of "the black stuff," Guinness. It's actually a deep red, if you can find enough light within the pub smoke to see it. He pulls a chair up to the cluster of players and lifts his guitar from its case.

I watch those strong, lean arms, the ones which hold me so lovingly, now cradling the instrument. He takes on his music-concentration expression, brow slightly furrowed, gaze on the strings, mouth set straight and tight. I've suggested to him and his bandmates to smile at their audience, as do the pros, but that must take veteran-grade skill. At least he doesn't grimace as if inhaling sauerkraut, and stick his tongue tip out between his lips, as did one of his former music partners.

While Bruce is immersed in his nirvana, I'm happy to sit, sip "minerals" (soda), tap my foot, people-watch, and people-listen. I bring out my paper pad, pens, and watercolor crayons; first I sketch, and then I use tiny, wetted brushes to smooth and blend, which turns the crayoning painterly. My art distracts me from the smoke stink. It also gives me an excuse to stare at the characters around me, who sporadically raise their mugs and shout out *sláinte (SLAWN shuh)*, cheer. My pad is palm-sized, so I can easily keep private my more unfortunate results. Many a curious pubber approaches to sneak peeks and tell me of their lives and loves, travels and travails. (I'll bet that even if I were nodding off, they would proffer their stories anyway—more than do the musicians, drinkers seem to require a bit of an audience. I wonder if *gregarious* and *chummy* are Irish words.)

A skinny man with a well-worn face, wearing a crumply, gray, stained Jeff cap and tarnished-white hair down past his shoulders, says to me "Where are yeh from?"

"America."

"Well, I know that," he says. "But where?"

"Oregon."

"Oregon," he repeats. "That's where the Oregon Trail started from."

"It's actually where the Oregon Trail ended up."

"Yeah, well," he shrugs. "It must be a lot like Ireland,

Oregon: a lotta music. Everyone on the Oregon Trail brought along their instruments, and so they all got there and make a lotta music from all over."

"Yep," I say. "It's a lot like Ireland, a lot of music, and it's beautiful too, and the weather."

He says, "Oh, *here* it rains all the time."

I don't bother to explain that in our valley, it rains day and night most of each soggy year.

Wondering about his atypical accent, I ask, "Where are *you* from?"

"I live here."

"And are you *from* here?"

His scowl deepens. "That's complicated. I've lived here *tirty*-one years, but I wasn't born in this country. This is a strange place to live, and a hard place."

Thirty-one years ago he came—that was the late 60s. I think of the far-flung wanderings of our generation. A saying Bruce still quotes from that era, by The Firesign Theater comedy troupe: "How can you be in two places at once, when you're not anywhere at all?"

This man is asking, "Do you have a daughter?"

"Yes, one."

"Well, if her looks take after her mother, she's done quite well for herself."

Not knowing what to do with that, I change tracks: "How do you make a living?"

"Well I play music every night. An' work in a kitchen all summer." He shakes his head, "It's hard, it's hard."

"This seems to be a pub for young people. Are all pubs like that?"

He answers, "Saturday night all over the world it's the same. London or Paris or Switzerland, or, or, everywhere,

Saturday night it's the same thing."

He turns and heads to the bar. I look back to the musicians just as one is sticking a leg out straight, the gesture I know is the code to end a tune or set.

Feckin' Brilliant

In the past few years, Bruce has thrilled himself adopting several speech mannerisms from Irish acquaintances and friends. He'll say, "Let's go to that show Friday-a-week."

"Huh? You mean a week from Friday, right?"

He'll say, "It's half-two already."

"No. It's two-thirty. Speak English, Bruce."

Here, it hasn't taken long for me to hear my *own* speech slipping into what I think is authentic. I'm absorbing every splendid nuance. The Irish brogue, Irish phrasing, Irish vocabulary pour from my tongue as fluidly as Guinness from the tap—at least as *I* hear myself. I could pass for a feckin' *native*, I'm sure, especially were I to dye my hair. (Not really. As mentioned previously, there's something that tips off the residents. A pheromone? A Celtic sixth sense?)

I've identified what seem to be the key Irish adjectives, and I fall in love with them:

Lovely   Grand   Splendid   Brilliant

Of course, these very words have always been available in our own version of the language, but they are under-utilized in the United States. In Ireland, all you need is one of them to cover any situation.

Okay, I'm exaggerating—a tendency I must have picked up from Irish storytellers, drunks, and run-of-the-mill braggarts. One additional adjective does jigs throughout their speech: *feckin'*

Bruce and I watched many an Irish movie before this trip, including *The Commitments, The Secrets of Roan Inish, Dancing at Lughnasa,* and *My Left Foot.* Because their dialogues were at break-neck speed, and they lacked subtitles, we'd whisper to each other, "*What* did he say?" "Did *you* catch that?" We and the other Americans in the theaters answered, "I dunno." Only from the facial expressions of the actors did we get the gist of who was poor and who was drunk, who was sad and who desperate.

Except we did understand *feckin'*. That word came through clear as the glister of red hair. According to our sampling of the film industry, few things Irish have any attribute other than *feckin'*.

Here in the real-life country itself, the atmosphere in the pubs is indeed an amalgamate of smoke with generous splatters of *feckin'*.

Yet *I* am not directly asked whether I'd like some *feckin'* Guinness, nor told that the restroom is around the *feckin'* corner, nor am I informed the session is a *feckin'* good one. Maybe these Catholics walk on eggshells near American women.

Anyway, I learn to speak in the vernacular.

"Do yeh take milk in yer tea?" "Yes, please, milk would be *lovely*."

"What'd yeh think of the Moore Street market?" "*Brilliant; brilliant* indeed."

"How was yer stroll along the Liffey?" "Ah, 'twas *grand*, 'twas *grand*."

"Is the breakfast to yer liking?" "The breakfast is *splendid*." ("But," I don't say, "We won't be needing any more of yer *feckin'* toast, thank you.")

I nail it brilliantly, if I do say so *meself*.

The Poetry of the Map: Select Irish Town Names

I never tire of reading them aloud:
Ringaskiddy   Skibbereen   Cork   Blarney
Just listen:
   Bantry Bay   Glandore   Clona Kitty
         Drimoleague   Knockraha
And these:
   Glanmire   Sallybrook   Balyduff
How about:
   Ballyhooly   Casteltownroche   Tipperary   Leap
And more, so many more. *Watergrasshill*—wouldn't I love
to state that as my home town. (Yet we do live in Corvallis,
which is twisted French for "Heart of the Valley." Not bad.)

   Truly, it's pure poetry. Music to the ears, it is.

Jana Zvibleman

Castles on the Ground

We drive past a castle here and a castle there. They're considered a major attraction, but neither of us is feeling it. Eventually we decide we *should* check out one, since they've been waiting for us for centuries.

Approaching *Ballahooligrowltarffifmiclancytoorah*, or whatever this imposing structure is, we meet steps. Many, many, many gray stone steps. To where? Dark, dank towers? Rat fiestas and torture chambers? We aren't tempted to climb. Nor are we keen on paying the *punts* required for admission to grimness. So we enter only the free, ground-level, dim, royal gift shop and search for treasures therein. Well, you can look at only so many leprechaun-encrusted potholders and shamrock-shaped key chains and Guinness postcards. The only pots of gold here are printed on green sweatshirts that cost a kettleful.

A day later, being good sports, we try a different castle shop. Same commercial clichés.

So for most of our trip, it suffices to merely point at another turreted silhouette on the horizon, and yet another. In days of yore, Irish kings must've been thick as thieves. Our best use of these monuments is as a backdrop to our picnics. When we peasants need to stretch and refresh, we often find the neighborhood castle, park our rented donkey cart, and plunk down on the genteel grounds to be sated by our loaf of bread and jug of wine, or rather, our apples, cheese, and crackers.

More Pub Talk

At Long's Pub on the Dingle Peninsula, I'm concentrating on my sketch of a girl with long red braids who's singing and playing a concertina in the particularly lively session. I notice that two middle-aged fellows near her are staring at me. The small-headed, big-bodied one leans his head towards his short, skinny, bald buddy and they converse. Then the big guy rises to his feet, Guinness in-hand, and lumbers my way.

"Me friend says yeh're drawing me. An' he says yeh'd better use two pieces of paper to get me all in!"

He and his drink shake with his laughter.

I feel obliged to tell him that I was actually drawing the squeeze-box player. Sagging as if disappointed, he shows no interest in viewing my picture, and he returns to his seat. I switch to him as my model. I manage to fit him, complete with his belly *and* his Guinness *and* his stool, *and* the fireplace *and* window *and* the curtains, *as well as* Bruce in the foreground, all within the four-by-five-inch page. As I'm adding just a few more strokes of hair on his head, thinking of bringing my picture over to show him, he stumbles towards and out the pub door.

Fungie in Dingle

Our friend Catherine, she-who-desires-the-American-pizza-stone, arranged for us to rendezvous in Dingle.

Dingle. A name which tickles. It's a town of taprooms, full to the rim with tourists on pub crawls. At the Dingle Harbour, we're happily entertained by people and boats. This place is heralded as the "Embarkation Point for The Blasket Islands." At their population peak in 1916, the Blaskets claimed 176 fish-and-potato eaters; by 1956 they were abandoned. They remain uninhabited by humans, overrun by rabbits. The multicolored pamphlets shouting from Dingle kiosks fail to entice us to the islands. Nor do the watercraft of every color of the rainbow, continuously bobbing for paying passengers.

The tour boats troll also for the Fungie-curious. Pronounced *FUNJ ee*, the bottlenose dolphin has frolicked in these waters since 1983. He's a rare "solitary-sociable cetacean," beloved for his friendliness to humans, some of whom jump in to swim with him. More board the boats, cameras cocked, eager for the thrill of seeing Fungie leap into the air, looking for all the world like he's smiling. We decide against embarking and merely visit the landlocked bronze sculpture of the mascot; on it climb a tidal wave of children.

While we are here, seems there are no real-Fungie sightings. We wonder whether he's merely mythical. In-the-flesh or not, he's the mainstay of Dingle's economy, evidenced by the clatter of shops hyping Fungie key chains, posters, plastic replicas, and tickets for the viewing boats.

Our Very Own Redheads

We hang around in Dingle, scanning the scene not for the dolphin but for our friends, whom we haven't been with in a *donkey's age*. Finally, we hear "Bruce! Jana!" and out of the throng of redheads, four emerge and move towards us, Fungie-sized smiles on their faces. We share warm, enthusiastic hugs with Catherine, a broad-faced, strong-looking beauty with long, flame-colored curls, and Rory, wiry and pale with squinty eyes, a twisted grin, and hair the reddish-brown of a penny that's been around-the-block. Lester is all freckles and eight-year-old bursts; Fiona, three, is a button-cute chunk of giggles. The kids tug us all to the Fungie statue, which they scale. Soon we parade to our car and then theirs, at last off-loading one pizza stone, one tackle box.

Jana Zvibleman

Ireland is a Small Town, or, I Only Know What I Heard

Lingering together in Fungie-land, we are happy to explore inside a bookstore. I'm glad the campaign to reclaim the native language does not yet dominate. Selfish, I know, but it's more fun for me to browse through titles I can decipher.

I find the section of books *about* Ireland, where a particular one calls to me. It's thick with the collected stories of Eamon Kelly who, the jacket cover claims, is Ireland's "master storyteller." That's a big deal in a land where storytelling is paramount. A teller is a *seanchai*; Eamon Kelly is THE *seanchai*.

His story titles themselves entice me, including "The Hereafter," "Con and Bridgie," "Mick the Fiddler Comes Home," "Pegg the Damsel," "The Barefooted Gandor," "Filling the Firkins," and "Washing the Cock's Feet."

The first paragraph of the first story in the collection goes like this:

"My father never took off his hat except when he was going to bed and into Mass, and my mother said he slept in the two places."

I'm hooked, which apparently does not surprise Eamon Kelly—I note his amused gaze from the forest-green book cover. He's comfortable as an old lamb in his woolen vest and fedora, his mouth open mid-tale.

When I show the book to Catherine, she says, "Yeah, Eamon Kelly, a'course." She used to date his grandson, and thus she met the man himself on several occasions. To our disappointment, she conjures no up-close-and-personal anecdotes, reporting merely, "He was so funny! Just so funny!"

We take Eamon with us, and for the rest of our travels he's our nighttime reading to each other. We learn the *seanchai*, born in 1914 and still with us, is indeed widely beloved by his people. They put his telling on the radio and they put his telling on the television; they set him down live on the stage for the telling.

The last lines of the last paragraph of the last story in this collection goes like this:

> " . . . they crossed over the stepping stones and I came by the bridge, they were drowned and I was saved and all I ever got for my storytelling was shoes of brown paper and stockings of thick milk. I only know what I heard, I only heard what was said and a lot of what was said was made up to pass the night away!"

Archways

I've disparaged the rural roads here—their narrowness, lack of peripheral views, gutted surfaces. Yet occasionally, listening to *trad* music on the radio, singing along with my dear chauffeur, I relax and appreciate the sylvan charm. No demanding traffic signals. No horns. No sirens, rude maniacs, billboards.

The sweetest feature of many a *boreen* is the arch above. Trees on each side have been allowed to spread their branches, so they reach each other with grace, creating a leafy tunnel, a magical passage toward our next discoveries.

Of Skibbereen

We follow our redheads south and farther to the tiny town whose name, *On Sciobairin,* means little boat harbor. (Its English name, Skibbereen, brings to my mind the pet turtle, Skipperdee, in the children's picture book *Eloise.* How could one not be tickled by such fun sounds?) In a short time we're zoomed back centuries, to the rural outskirts where Rory and Catherine are trying their soft hands at being *culchies:* country-dwellers.

Their current home is an aged farmhouse, an old, old *gaff* (*European* old, not old as in parts of the U.S. where a building half my age may be deemed *historic.*) This is of the local country style, stone walls thick enough in which to stash that pot of gold.

With the rental of this house, they inherited a border collie. No sooner do we start looking around, Lester drags us to the rear mud room to view her newborn passel of pups. Wrinkly, squiggly, plump. Eight of them, not quite as many as there are freckles on Lester's nose. What's the vernacular for *cute, cute, cute*?

Back in the main room, seeing the stone fireplace, I ask, "Do you use peat?"

"*Turf,* ah, sure," Rory says. "An' I've got some here. Are yeh after a fire? I'll build a savage whopper for yeh."

We've read about the centuries-old practice of harvesting a layer of long-decaying vegetation from bogs. On our way to Skibbereen, we passed a field in which several people were bent over doing just that. Hand-hoed strips are dried and cut to rough, dark, earthen chunks. Modern industry uses tractors; the scraped peat is shredded and compressed into briquettes. I imagine the world's remaining trees leading a campaign to save themselves: "Use turf! Not wood!"

Soon, lounging on the wide window sills, feeling the fire's warmth, we find it's true that this fuel is smokeless and slow-burning; its aroma is, not surprisingly, earthy. A foreignish earth. Strangely pleasing.

Though these folks are toying with traditional Irish ways, they're young, modern, and have spent time in the States. Catherine wears *au courant* clothes. I suspect Rory would not know a ewe from a sow. Lester shows off his Japanese Pokémon card collection. Fiona wants us to join in play with her Barbies; she's arranging them on a cushion bought in Oregon, probably made in Taiwan.

Yet this is their real Irish home. It's a privilege to be in it with this family, grand fun hanging out with them. During our first cozy dinner together, which is delicious fish potato pie, we catch them up on mutual Oregon friends and recount our travels so far. Our directional mishap on the "Jewel Carrich Way" is a big hit, Rory hooting with laughter that we "probably *went in aresways*." After warm strawberry raspberry crumble, Bruce and I read aloud to the kids. Then Catherine and Rory show us their plans for building an attached house on the east side for her Mother and Dad—that for sure shows them to be more trad Irish than modern American.

At every chance, Rory amuses himself by spinning yarns of his drinking escapades, splashed with guffaws: "Me mate was so knackered he tumbled arseways into a priest-ridden buildin', and me followin'!" and "I was polluted from now till the cows come home, but here the cows a'course turn out to be bulls an' . . . . . " We've heard it all before, or versions thereof, when he was in the States.

As during most of his monologues, Catherine now just rolls her eyes, busies herself with the children; occasionally she *gives out* to Rory with mild scoldings.

For a break from his beer brags, I step outside to view the wide landscape, a soft, pastel quilt of hills and fields, with appliquéd trees and crops. A gate hangs open; cats squabble; blossoms close. The moon is up, a waxing gibbous, and I think about it being the same moon our friends far away are seeing. It's said plants communicate with their kind all over the earth. I think of the grass here speaking to the grass at our home, sharing this moment's message that all is well.

Back in Western Oregon, Catherine had expressed dismay at "the lack of twilight," observing, "In America it goes just from day to night. Day. Night." I now *get* what she meant. Here the evening approaches gradually, the light lingering like the vibrations of harp strings, offering a long trilling to accompany the letting-go of day. It's a sweet, leisurely transition, a time think back on one's worldly doings, and now to settle into this full moment.

I look toward the nearest other farmhouse, which in our world might be the distance away of six blocks, maybe more. To the side of that house is a field, and in the center of that is a circle of stacks of huge hay bales. From this view, I could measure each stack as the height of my thumb. They dwarf the stout farmer hoisting himself on and off a faded-green tractor. Atop this haystack and that, children are dancing and goofing. Several are the size of my thumbnail, one the size of my pinky nail. One child leaps now from one pile to the next, to the next; another child catches up, climbing to that bale, that one; the next child, smaller and clumsier, clambers behind; and so goes their spiraling play.

The twilight breezes from there to here, wafting over trees, ignoring human boundaries. I think, this air has never been inhaled before. No, that can't be right—rather, it's the same breathed by local lads and lasses, grasses, trees, of countless generations. Now it carries wisps of those children's calls and laughs. Wish I could tuck this pastoral scene in my pocket and carry it always. Wouldn't it be nice if that disgruntled man in Ennistymon could be transported here, now.

"Those are the Fitzgeralds." Catherine has appeared next to me. "The *da* is Eamon. The children are Clare, age ten; Richard, age eight; Colm, six; and Owen, four. The baby, Niall, would be inside now with Clare, the mum."

Catherine recounts that as soon as those kids spotted Lester moving in, they sent shouting invitations to him to join in their play, which he did eagerly. It was months before Lester could persuade Clare, Richard, and the rest to come visit *his* place. "They were so shy, we'd have to drag 'em over, and they'd cling to each other and stare at us and run back to home," Catherine laughs. "They have no fears at all there on their own turf, but we were unfamiliar, and *still* it's very strange for them to come so far away."

Two Litters

Catherine has made Lester leave the new puppies in peace, but one afternoon she determines they're ready to tolerate company. At her "All right, then," Lester takes off leaping and hopping through the grasses, screeching to the Fitzgeralds, "Come see! Come see!"

Bruce and I are just as excited as Lester at the prospect of being with more children. Through our Montessori training and experience, we've gained insights into early human development; young ones' *zest for life* is the premier characteristic that sparks the same in us. Bruce especially shines with humor and creativity while with children. The year he "graduated" from classroom Guide to Head of School, he took to wearing a necktie, "So people can tell me from the children," he said. (And yet, several of the boys then would show up at school wearing their own little neckties, to emulate Bruce.)

Now in two shakes of a puppy tail, Lester and all but the babe-in-arms are tumbling onto the back porch. The Fitzgeralds cling together, fixing their huge eyes on the litter. Bruce points out the tails, and asks the children to wag theirs, which brings them to giggling ease. He encourages them to pick up a pup each. We're thrilled to capture images of these freckled boys and girls with the spotted sheepdog pups, all one-hundred-percent Irish and wriggling.

Come On!

In the evening, Lester asks me, "What do you like to do?"
"I like to look at flowers."

"We have lots of dandelions. And foxgloves. What else do you like to do?"

"I like to take walks."

"Yes, we can take walks. Do you like Pokémon?"

"No, I do not like Pokémon."

"Well do you like the pictures of Pokémon? You would like the Fox with Nine Tails, and you would like the Crab, and you would like . . .."

"I like to read books."

"Do you like to climb trees?"

"Yes, I like to climb trees."

"Well we can read my stories up in my special climbing place. Come on!"

His Mom says, "No, Lester, too late. To bed with yeh."

The Cock of Skibbereen

*E*E-AW   *EEEE-AAAW*
        Attack on my sleep.

After drowsy moments of wondering what primeval monster is *EE-AW* dying of childbirth in *EEE-AAW* a train wreck . . .

Consciousness dawns, so to speak, on me: It's crazy early in the morning, I'm in some foreign countryside, and it's a beast I'm hearing. *EE-AW. EEE-AAW*

I've never heard this sound before in person, yet I've sung "Old MacDonald" and read aloud picture books of animal babies enough times, I can identify a mule. Or is it a donkey? *EE-AWW*

Yet this sound seems a caricature. *EE-AW. EEEE-AAAW* It's raw, rude, brash, bizarre. A noise to which no kindly mother nor preschool teacher would ever expose a sensitive young child. *EEE-AAW.*

Silence. I wait on alert, strangely eager to hear it again.

I rise and pad to the window; in the golden light, I scan the fields around. A *boreen*, three fields, and a farmhouse away, I spy the hairy beast: actual enough, yet it also *looks* like a caricature. I wonder whether the Irish ass is different than the American.

Behind me, on the bed, Bruce slumbers through pastoral silence and commotion, emitting his own beastly music.

Story in a Tree

The one bathroom's occupied, so I wander outside. White sky, as at home. Grasses, cows and cows. I have a satisfying pee, privately, out by the fuchsia hedges and heal-all plants, then wander back. Here's Lester, in his striped pjs, holding his bowl of dry cornflakes and the book of fables he wanted to read with us last night. He's looking at me with wide longing eyes, saying he'll take me to his special climbing place. I say, "I'll have to go in and get my glasses. Or you'll have to be our reader."

"I'll read to you," he says, and I follow him down a steep slope, avoiding only *some* of the nettles, to a huge felled ash tree. Now we're climbing onto the diagonal trunk, from one haphazard branch to another. We both find spots warmed already by the sun and good fits for our different bottoms, and we settle.

I adore his freckled intensity as he reads, in his Irish brogue and his Lester lisp, of the three daughters who one-by-one set out to seek their fortunes. He stumbles on the word "washerwoman," then gets through that to the fact she's a witch. The youngest daughter is carried by the black bull whose brothers are men in castles. I hold Lester's bowl of cornflakes; without looking up, he periodically reaches and grabs a handful that becomes a mouthful, still reading, each word now crunchy.

"Lester!" we hear, and up the slope in blue satin pajamas, clutching her own bowl, is his little sister.

Lester calls, "Fiona, do *yeh* need help?" My heart is warmed.

She nods. He calls, "Just a moment," reads another paragraph, then hops down off the tree and runs to her, gets her onto his back and carries her down through the roughest of the terrain. He unloads her onto a low, wide branch and climbs back up. She laughs through her mouthful of flakes and gazes up at him intently, as he reads along, all the way to "And they're still living happily ever after, as far as I know."

We all climb down to the turf, hearing moos plus the *grorrwwrrs* of a power saw, and back up to the house for proper breakfast.

The Extreme Edge

Catherine says, "Let's go to the beach, then." Our own northwest coast is a place of beauty, but it is reliably chilly. Lounging on the sand there would usually be *cloud*bathing, and jumping into the waves is only for nutsy Polar Bear Clubbers. Now as we head out, we don't know whether to expect that or the Floridian beach scene of Bruce's childhood.

The Mizen Head beach area does indeed share Oregon's chill, and it is windy, and people-y. A man is zoodle-doodling on an accordion wider than a passing ship. Children and adults chase, yell, jump, screech, tumble on the sand; a few, but only a few, bob in the water.

I try molding damp sand into a three-dimensional rendition of a Celtic knot. I scrabble my fingers to dig the *unders* and pile the *overs*—until the sea waves my lumpy mounds away.

The wind becomes more bold, eager to play with the fringe of my rainbow-striped scarf, so I take it from around my neck. Keeping hold of the cloth, I let it be tugged and flapped. Then gripping each end with a fist, I hold it high so it becomes an animated arch; with it and the wind, I swoosh, twirl, and dance.

This is the southernmost tip of Ireland; they call it the *extreme edge.* Catherine says it was the last home ground many an emigrant touched before sailing away. I've not visited the shores where each of my grandparents departed from *their* longtime homelands. As beleaguered Jews, like many a beleaguered Irish person, they also had to conjure up the nervous *chutzpah* to flee, so they and their progeny might survive in a remote unknown. Here

I stare out over red hair curls on the beach, farther to liquid waves, to the horizon, picturing brave and terrified individuals clutching ragged bags, brave and terrified families clutching each other, taking final looks back. I imagine them spotting back on the shore the vision of a rainbow scarf waving, "Fare-thee-well in the *beyont*."

Irish Cuisine, So-to-Speak

Our first morning in this country, we were surprised but didn't pay it much mind, so jet-dazed we didn't have expectations of whatever food was placed in front of us. At our second breakfast, we assumed it an oversight, or a clue we had chosen inferior establishments. By our third, we figure out it must be intentional: toast in Ireland is not *toasty*. Room-temperature yet scorched-looking bread seems to be considered integral to a civilized breakfast. I trust you understand what is wrong with this picture.

Almost every B&B dining table includes a chrome rack, and in the slots each morning stand upright thin slices. On the occasional table lacking such a rack, the same sorry stuff lies in a basket, ungraciously piled on top of quite nice brown bread.

From no typical Irish kitchen does that familiar toast aroma waft, seducing one out of bed. We think the faux crisping may be attempted off-premises, possibly delivered weekly from each town's Limp Toast Bakery. Or, maybe native engineers have developed a handy home appliance which accepts an innocent slice of white bread and *sans* heat coats it with a charr-y facade. (Except, of course, for the blessed Craggy, lauded previously.)

At the usual Irish tables, no melting of creamy liquid gold, soaking into crisp warm crumbs. Instead, butter must be shoved along the slice's impersonal surface. The so-called *spread* remains in its solid state, alerting the partaker to how the intact dairy slab will settle in her or his arteries.

So what's the point of toast then?

Toast pushed aside, Bruce and I remain curious about true Irish meals. Catherine educates us quickly that corned beef and cabbage is *not* one of them. "*Nobody* here eats that," she says, with an attitude. I think of the deli corned-beef sandwiches that flavored *our* youths. No cabbage with it; wait, actually, there was sauerkraut.

Catherine adds, "We do have bacon—*ham* to you—and cabbage." Because Bruce and I are veggie-sticklers, we miss out on that.

Not to mention black pudding, which Rory makes sure to mention. One day, he barrels into their home pleased-as-punch to have brought a parcel of it. Pudding is one of my favorite comfort foods, so I join in his excitement, until Catherine explains why this particular gift from the Celts is black. (I can't bring myself to share details with you.) Although not taking the hint of my expression, she goes on (and here I must point out that Catherine has kissed the Blarney Stone more than once) about why it's not actually *called* blood pudding.

She adds: Irish black pudding is closely related to the beloved Scottish *haggis*. I was in the vicinity of one of *those* once in my life, which was more than enough, thank you.

We're faced with certain other mammalian treasures such as Irish stew, reportedly seeped in Guinness plus other, indeterminate, ingredients. Though it's a cultural *must*, we don't indulge. Rory dismisses us with "Away on!" (You can't be serious; get outta here!) and an eye-rolling "Aye sure why nat?" (To each his own, or somesuch.) The countryside's cows and sheep, however, thank us.

Rory and Catherine decide to take us to their favorite local restaurant. When in Rome . . . so we go dining out with the native Irish, at a *pizzeria*. To be charitable, I could say Skibbereen pizza holds its own—but only compared to America's cardboard-pizza chains and frozen imitations.

Here, pizza is accompanied of course by Guinness.

Most days on our own, Bruce and I stop at little shops for simple fare to tote on our excursions. At one outdoor farmer's market, we purchase the tastiest protein we've found so far in Ireland: cheese from France, with *herbs de Provence*. Oh, there is also Catherine's fish potato pie, plus the sumptuous feast she makes for my birthday, with several non-carnivorous recipes from her cookbook by Jamie Oliver, a Brit.

Holding hands and daydreaming along a street one evening, Bruce and I get a food review by a passing group of loud young adults. "I declare *that there* The Worst Hamburger in the Whole World!" one shouts.

Another responds, "Yer right, there. Though better than feckin' MecDonalds!"

Still More Pub Talk

Throughout our travels, the weather is a popular topic of conversation. Deep inside the dank dark of the pubs, far from sky and air, the locals love to brag or complain about outside.

On one sunny day, a man tells us, "Don't take our good weather away."

"We brought it," I counter.

"Ah, then thank you, yes."

Eavesdropping on the pubs' publics, I figure I'm not being rude. Mashed together as we are, no one could expect an intimate *tête-à-tête*. I am of the opinion that we are all playing character parts in a grand performance.

Among my overheard souvenirs: Two young women are enthusiastically shouting advice to the lovelorn, a third woman.

"But watch it. He's a young chap not quite sure of himself, yeh know."

"Listen, it's like a dog yeh want to come to yeh. If you chase it, it's the worse *ting* yeh can do. It will just run away. But, if yeh ignore it . . .!"

"Ignore it!" all three proclaim, raising their glasses high.

In one pub, the *session* takes a break, hauling off their chairs and gear to make room on the wooden riser for a batch of pubescent girls dressed in identical green, orange, and white frocks with short flouncy skirts. White socks cling up towards their bony knees; heavy black shoes make quite the clatter. We recognize the dance from a few accidental encounters in the States with performances by daughters of friends. No, it's not to our taste, the regimented high-steps, grim, stiff faces, rigid arms and paralyzed upper bodies.

Seems closer to military marching than to the fluidity of dance. We've also endured long minutes of "Riverdance" before we could change the channel. We do appreciate that these girls are trained well. Applause, cheers. Back to the *session*, please!

In a Name

Bruce proclaims he's no longer to be called *Bruce*. He's going to take on an Irish name. Thus begins a lively discussion among all of us, including the children. Names, commentaries, and protests fly. Bruce decides he's *Liam*; the crowd insists on *Griffin* instead; no, no, he looks like a *Fergal*.

"Fiona, what shall we call Bruce?"

"Bruce!"

Lester, giggling, contributes "*Bowser.*"

Finally *Kierán (KEE* run*)* sticks. Catherine tells us the spelling requires a *fada* on the "a": we save till another time asking what in the world a *fada* may be. All that evening and the next two days, it's "Another Guiness for you, *Kierán*?" and "Nice tune, *Kierán*," and *Kierán* this and *Kierán* that and *Kierán* the other. When we remember.

To join the trend, I sort through female names. My authorities tell me that my first choice, *Fada,* is not an acceptable name; it's not a name at all. Fiona says to call me *Fiona*; her mother says that's taken. My Jewish upbringing precludes my becoming a *Mary*. *Gráinne,* is put forth; I don't like the sound, *Grawn-ya*. This is a big decision. After much deliberation, I disclose, "I'll be *Siobhan (shuv ON.)*"

Rory snorts, chokes on his beer. "Ah, no! Not *Siobhan.* "

"Why's that?" I ask. "I kinda like it. Like a fluffy dessert, or a sheer fabric."

He's laughing his red head off. "Yeh'll have a hard time of it, yeh will!"

Catherine wags her finger at him, as she also snickers.

Rory pauses howling to explain: "When we were in school, the girls named *Siobhan*, we always teased them wit' 'Siobhan yer knickers, yer Mammy's comin'!'"

My buddy *Kierán* is greatly amused, to Rory's gratification.

I stick with *Jana*.

Bird's in a Tin

We pack into the car with Catherine and the kids for her errands. Bumping along the *boreen*, she stops to chat with the occasional neighbor strolling or working outside. Mrs. Sheeran, a huge, shaggy-haired woman dragged by her huge, shaggy-haired dog, tells Catherine, "Do come by anytime for a *cuppa*."

Mairead and Oisin, an aged couple, are about to enter their gate, one using a walker, the other a cane. Catherine asks whether there's any nice *ting* they'd like picked up for them from town. Oisin chuckles, "Sure and I'd like a pair a' new legs, if yeh can manage it. I'll put 'em to good use, I will."

After we pass them, Catherine says to us, "An' yeh noticed, Oisin has the map of Ireland on his face, my mother would say."

"Mm-hmm," I mumble, though I'm not sure what she means. The man did look *very* Irish, I guess. Wool cap, wool vest. His face? Well, wrinkles. Did they literally mimic the geography of this country? Got *me*.

Farther along the rural road, a young man in shirt-sleeves directs his greeting to me and *Kierán*: "Ah, here to locate the restin' place of yer dear Irish great-granny, are yehs? All the Americans do."

In town, Catherine parks the car on the supermarket lot, which is small but disappointingly non-quaint: asphalt, signs, light poles. As she and the kids get out and move ahead of us, I call her name, mime that she's left her wallet on the dashboard; I catch up to whisper, "The car's unlocked!"

She shrugs, "It's fine, I've in my pocket what money I'll need for now." Bruce — I mean *Kierán*—and I look at each other, shrug too, and follow along.

In the store, Lester and Fiona trail their mother as she selects staples for their household. *Kierán* and I meander the aisles sightseeing, picking off shelves curiosities we won't find at home: here's a mix for brown bread; let's try this sheep cheese, and this one. How about Bewley's Irish Breakfast Tea, by Bewleys of Grafton Street, Dublin?

Oh, Bird's Custard Powder, Original Flavour. Catherine had said she'll put it between layers of the birthday cake she'll make for me, that Bird's is the finest, richest, creamiest, eggy-est custard. Yet this red, yellow, and blue tin claims as the only ingredients cornflour, salt, flavourings, and colour. If we were curious enough about the chemistry, we could send an email inquiry to krafteurope.com. Boring old *Kraft*, is it? Oh well, let's try it.

We bring our discoveries to the cart holding their cereal, milk, fruit, vegetables. Soon we toss in Cadbury chocolate bars. Catherine had educated us in the States: though the brand's widely available, it's manufactured by Hershey, and thus is *terrible* anywhere but Ireland. Since it's an essential, whenever she ventures from home shores, she packs *authentic* Cadbury's, made in Coolack, Dublin. When in danger of running out, she makes urgent overseas calls imploring relatives to ship a resupply. Today, here, the product happens to be *on special*: buy three six-inch bars of any variety and get a plastic bag of ten for free. Bruce—oh, you know who I mean—and I take our time considering the options; we gather up Dark Chocolate with Nuts, Milk Chocolate Rum & Raisin, and Plain Milk Chocolate. The wrappers brag, "Cadbury milk chocolate contains a glass and a half of cream in every half pound," illustrated by drinking glasses floating above a hunk of candy, pouring down thick, pure-white streams. Seems folks here are not obsessed with weight loss nor cholesterol counts.

When we've exhausted our acquisitive urge, we check out and arrange the goodies into cloth bags. The store sells them cheap, urging their re-use; as Oregonians who habitually recycle, Bruce and I feel kinship with Skibbereen-ites saving the earth. We load the bags into the cart, which Catherine wheels toward the entryway. But she stops before the door, parking the cart by the inside wall, parallel to nine carts also full of purchases. She takes Fiona's hand and heads out, saying over her shoulder, "Now, shall we go to the library or the art gallery?"

"Catherine, the *groceries*?"

She chuckles. "We don't want to be lugging all that around town, do we?"

"So we'll lock them in the car?"

"Nah. They'll wait right there."

Kierán and I look back, bidding farewell to our treats. What distinguishes our cart from the others, and what could possibly protect them from rogue chocolate-thieves?

Upon our return an hour and a half later, Bruce/*Kierán* and I are ecstatic to see our groceries awaiting us, untouched. We all celebrate with several flavours of Cadbury's.

Art-Romping

Who would have thought to find in remote Skibbereen a gallery with quality contemporary paintings? Art displays are a home to me. I drink up creative *juices* from good art. And I like the backdrop of both museums and galleries to make photographs, usually of Bruce, often of strangers. I especially relish capturing viewers in postures, colors, and styles which serendipitously coordinate with the featured paintings, prints, and sculptures.

Today we thrill to huge, colorful abstracts, reminiscent of finger paintings, in an airy, modern room. The splashiness of colors, especially reds, plus the open floor space invite squiggly-haired, stubby-legged Fiona to romp and run, her round-cheeked, laughing face turned toward my adoring camera.

Sweet Glandore

Far from my birthplace, it's my birthday. *Kierán* and I venture out alone and drive into the town of Glandore, which the Irish says is Cuan Dor. Outside above two bays, at a small round table, we're loving the sun, entertained by the sailboats on blue water, sharing a prawn salad that includes slices of kiwi, orange, casaba melon, and strawberries, with brown bread. I'm indulging in sparkling lemonade in a graceful glass. *Yer man* is sipping Guinness with a shot of *crème de cassis*, which is blackcurrant liqueur—it's his recent discovery and drink of choice. Bartenders here know the concoction well; Catherine has called *Kierán* a "heathen" for it; we don't understand why.

This is a delectable moment to prolong. When our plates are empty, we go back into the café across the way to snag warm Irish soda bread and to telephone Rory and Catherine. "You *must* come meet us here." They already know Glandore. "But it's only fifteen minutes away!" Catherine doesn't want to delay her cooking and baking for my birthday. "Oh, but first it's lunchtime," we continue to press. "Just come for *part* of my birthday. And Catherine – you'll want to be wearing a dress-up hat! Maybe bring one for me too?"

While we await them, we spread butter and orange marmalade on the soda bread and make our most forward-thinking plan ever: we will commemorate our wedding's fiftieth anniversary on this very veranda. Whichever relatives and friends are still kicking in twenty-one years we'll invite to rejoice here with us. We have a somber moment as we think of our parents and other older loved ones who won't make it.

That leads us to memories of our strange wedding. The Hippies and the Families, we could title it. The rabbi was pleased to show how liberal he was by blessing a pair of long-haired kids. My mother was distraught at our friend showing up with three buddies, uninvited and unknown to us, all in their muddy communal-farm boots and overalls; my Uncle Irwin delighted in a long philosophical discussion with them. Bruce's Mom stomped in from across the country with Bruce's high school photo enshrined in her purse, to show her son short-haired and clean-cut, as he *really* was under all that hair; Mogen David and my Uncle Ralph worked on relaxing her a bit.

After the ceremony, Bruce and I were surprised by what someone declared a Jewish tradition: parents were set down on chairs and crowned with flower garlands, to celebrate their new status as empty-nesters. Around them circled the whole entourage: high-heeled aunts; gowned sisters; bouffant-haired cousins; me with my hair down to my waist and my flowing choir-like dress; Bruce with his mustache and muslin peasant shirt; uncles in suits and ties; freaks with long frowsy hair and beards. We all held hands and danced together.

Now in Glandore, we're an old married couple, still holding hands and still laughing about our wedding, when Rory, Catherine, Lester, and Fiona arrive like a bevy of twittering quail. We cheer. They also procure picture-worthy meals, and while eating, tell us the two bays are called Adam and Eve; boaters advise for safe passage, "Avoid Adam and Hug Eve." Rory is snickering, I'm sure conjuring up a bawdy image of this which, surprisingly, he doesn't verbalize, I assume because of the children.

Using our binoculars to scan the scene before us, Bruce—oh, yeah, *Kierán*— finds a large castle-y church-y building on a high hill, with much activity on its expansive grounds. We all are greatly entertained by passing the binoculars, witnessing some sort of party. Ah, the dressed-to-the nines, pastel guests, mingling on manicured lawns and wide porches.

The ladies wear wide-brimmed and wider-brimmed hats, large enough to be appreciated even at this distance with the naked eye; their long silky dresses float and waft. The men appear quite dapper, tailored and buffed in crisp grays and blacks, some with proper tophats. We see the glint of crystal stemware in gloved hands as people sip and give salutations, give salutations and sip, standing and strolling, in pairs and threes, reassembling and posturing in foursomes and large groupings, posing for portraits. Ah, there's a flouncy-white dress on a flouncy-white woman, the center of much attention. So this is a wedding reception. Enter the straight-backed groom with formal tails. More photo posing, with and without the blessed couple. Weaving throughout, white- and powder-blue-clothed children skip and tumble, run and flop.

Rory's running commentary is about which guest looks merely drunk and which *full-ossified*.

For respite from his monologue, I head to the restroom of *our* restaurant, wherein I find a framed poem by Rev. Dr. Patrick Aloysius Murray:

> "The gay, the beautiful, the grand
> Blending over wave and land
> The eye can ask no more
> Than it hath in sweet Glandore . . .
> Tree and flower, and sea and shore
> Thus live and breathe in sweet Glandore."

You said it, Patrick Aloysius! I walk back outside and inhale deeply, taking in even more of Glandore's ambience, which I'll call *delicious*, because it rhymes with Aloysius (maybe).

Oh Heavens No!

I can see that Rory is still at it, his hands gesturing, his *gob* yapping. It brings to mind an expression I picked up in a pub: that lad "can talk the hind legs off a donkey." Bruce is laughing, which I know encourages the blarney. I do at least appreciate Bruce's loyalty to friends and sweetness at overlooking their annoying ways.

(Yes, I'm back to calling him "Bruce." Maybe I am suffering mild culture-shock, but the heck with it, I'm more comfortable with the *feckin'* real name of my own true love.)

Instead of returning to Rory's *roryness*, I choose to amble down to the water's edge. Picking my way now from stone to stone over the shallows, I hear a greeting in a trill of a voice with a distinct accent. Ah: the Queen's English.

A stout woman introduces herself: "I see our secret Glandore has been discovered by America!"

I'm identified again, by looks alone. Curious. We chat. "Where are you staying?" I ask.

She points to a far hill and enunciates, "In the castle. My brother-in-law has the castle over there." She calls it *Kilforren*, or *Forkillen*, or . . . I'm distracted by her plethora of beaded necklaces, sparkly and matt; ivory, blue, yellow, green, orange; chokers and strands hanging down past her bosom, reaching her ample belly. Turning towards where she points, I say, "Ah, yes, the castle." I see nothing.

I wonder whether the British feel welcome in Ireland. How her brother-in-law came to acquire a piece of Irish soil. I ask instead, "What's it like inside? Dark and dank and cold?"

"Oh heavens no!" she says. "It's my brother's-in-law."

I'm pondering that when she adds, "It's all showers and curtains now."

Okay, then.

Of Blarney and Truth

The question is of eloquence, and whether or not the Blarney Stone, as the legend goes, truly gifts one with it.

Catherine becomes our tour guide to the Blarney Castle. She has us dodge the long stagnant line of tourists waiting to enter, and leads us around back, where we ascend 127 steps in the cram-your-shoulders staircase. We find ourselves high in the atmosphere, along the edges of the roof—and waiting in a different long stagnant line of tourists. We have time to gaze below at green gardens; I imagine quaint lawn games in days of yore, and whizzing arrows.

Bruce helps the hour pass by recounting a story of the poor *schlub* whose taxes were raised and therefore his survival threatened. His only option was to plead to the all-powerful lord of the land, which he feared to do, being a simple fellow and not much of a talker.

For some reason— I miss that part—the man kissed a boulder. It magically loosened his tongue, or oiled it, or made it honeyed, some metaphor showing that he was transformed into a *schmoozer.*

Of course, for the happy ending: the poor man's new-found eloquence successfully convinced Lord Moneybags to back off.

Speaking of blarney, I wonder where Bruce came up with that saga. Our guidebooks offer quite a different explanation of why people stand in line to kiss some rock.

To this day I still wonder which came first: "blarney" meaning exaggerated flattery or nonsense, or "baloney" as in "You're fulla baloney" and "Aw, baloney" and "I'm too polite to say *bullshit.*"

We reach the top. Now I get a good view of the sheer

drop, a black chasm, between the battlement on which we stand and the magic stone itself. Watching naive tourists in front of us risking their lives, I have to conjure self-magic to hold my tongue; I really want to say "No thank you" to the silly and death-defying experience. Yet, *what if*: maybe this ritual *will* make not only my mouth, but also my pen and my keyboard, fleet-of-foot so-to-speak. Might the language mastery promised amend for my never pursuing a certificate from the Iowa Writers Conference?

When we become the front lemmings on this precipice, a white-bearded, stout, rough-hewn man—a gargantuan leprechaun?—greets me graciously, though I am probably the 623rd ridiculous sightseer of his day. Maybe he's *Saint* Blarney. He coaches me in a kind voice: "Kiss the stone."

I hesitate again as I peer over, needing even more powerful magic now. *Jaysus*! I pray rapidly, "Please-grant-me-immunity-to-the-germs-carried-since-time-immemorial- from-every-land-on-earth, mingling,-thriving,-and-festering-on-this-moldy-geographic-feature."

The next challenge is the lying down on my back, hanging my head over the emptiness; now I offer a prayer that the old man be not only saintly but also strong as Lugh or some other Celtic superman. He bolts my legs down with his chunky hands, whilst I contort backwards. The absurd posture must have been thought up by some sadistic Irish tourism marketer. Or did Bruce's poor protagonist actually do it this way? Is this where the term "bending over backwards to please" comes from?

I do it.

In turns, so do we all. Not one of our party breaks a back nor falls into the valley of the Lee River. So, breathing again, we each toss *punt* into the muscle-man's donation basket; I am generous, figuring his insurance company must charge phenomenal rates for liability. I would be pleased if he'd spend a wee bit of his take on Lysol spray to occasionally disinfect the rock.

We retreat down the back stairs. At one level, a placard indicates the chamber of a lass of yore. We decide to snoop. In the grim, rugged enclosure, I try to imagine the life of a teenage girl, withering away within damp walls bare of music posters or snapshots of boys; nary an outlet for a hairdryer or screen.

We descend to *terra firma*, on which we spread our picnic. Soon all fears and doubts evaporate, as I find myself waxing melodiously on "our ascent up an infinitely whirling helix through the intimate chambers of the grand regal heart of the mystical Emerald Isle on the floriated grounds of this splendiferous citadel." I mention "the jeopardous solemnization we engaged in communally with the boulder of antiquity." I declare my name henceforth and forevermore to be *Ella Quince — get it?* I continue to postulate . . . until Catherine says, "*Jaysus*, shut up already. Here, eat a cookie."

Silenced of my blathering, I wonder whether the promise of the legend has indeed manifested within me. Or not.

Meanwhile, Catherine bids us to look *over there*.

The brother of hers with a degree in Irish history once directed her, as she now directs us, to consider the castle's exterior.

"Did yeh notice in the maid's chamber, the thick exterior wall? Do yeh remember how it sloped down to the little window?"

We do.

"Now do yeh see the dark markings streaking down the

outside from that window there and that one and that one too? The streaks that go all the way to the ground?" she says, pointing.

We do.

"And do yeh know what is the cause of that?"

We don't.

"Now do you see how lush is the foliage right there underneath each of those streaks?"

We do indeed.

"And so do yeh realize that there was no plumbing in the castle, and that the chambers had their little openings, and that those places show where the lord or lady, you know, did their business?"

Ah, we do realize that now, thank you, we do indeed.

Traveling Kisses

Speaking of Blarney-kissing . . .
I had never stepped foot beyond the Midwest when Bruce and I first met. Before long, we hitchhiked together from Wisconsin to California. Ever since, travel has been a shared pleasure, albeit limited by our jobs and wages. We managed via thumbs, boots, and worn-tread tires to make it across North America in various zig-zags, our itinerary usually inspired by the locations of family and friends.

I created my unique oral travelog, exclaiming to Bruce: *We're kissing in Kansas City! This is our first kiss in California/ North Dakota/ Florida!* So far, we've shared *besos* in as far away as Mexico and Ecuador.

Way over here in Europe, I again pick up the practice of proclaiming our kissing—I mean with each other, not the Blarney Stone. *A Cork kissing! We're kissing in Bantry Bay! Yay, now we've pashed and snogged across Ireland.* (I do hope those Irish slang words are family-friendly.)

Jana Zvibleman

Pub Talk, Continued

Most pub windows hold a sign, Children not allowed after 9 p.m. I'm not sure why. The Guinness flows around the clock. I observe just as many bleary-eyed men drooping on the bar stools at high noon as at midnight, blabbing just as loudly. I recite to myself the nursery rhyme, "Wee Willie Winkie runs through the town, Upstairs and downstairs in his nightgown. Rapping at the window, crying through the lock, 'Are the children in their beds, for now it's eight o'clock.'" It's Scottish, but that's okay; I'm impressed at my remembering the whole of it.

At one pub, a middle-aged woman with wild black hair sits alone under her personal blanket of smoke. All evening I've watched her lighting each new cigarette with the butt of her last one. Now she declares loudly, apparently to the whole planet, "Yeah, lads, I'm filling my nicotine prescription."

Taking another hard drag, she adds, "An' what do yeh need lungs for, anyway, really?"

It Was Here Without Us

*B*oíreann, which seems to be pronounced *BURR en*, is Irish for a rocky place or great rock (different from *boreen*, a narrow road). We hear about how amazing is The Burren on the west coast. Englishman Edmund Ludlow, who in the 1600s led a conquest of Ireland, declared the Burren "a country where there is not enough water to drown a man, wood enough to hang one, nor earth enough to bury him."

Because Ludlow was involved in the siege of *Limerick*, Bruce says it would've been brilliant had he instead said, "The Burren's a barren terrain/ for the Crown I fought for to gain. . . .." He gropes for next lines. Against my better judgment, I collaborate, to get it over with: "Though it had naught of wood, nor water nor good/ so the conquering's feckin' a pain." Our lil' limerick, fortunately, soon dissipates in the mist.

Anyway, I wonder what could be noteworthy about an expanse of rock, unless it were on the moon. Yet to oblige the travel-wise, we have arrived at Burren National Park.

The shop first. It peddles rocks and paintings of rockiness. In a display titled The Burren Exposure, with maps, old photos, and facts, one prominent quote enthralls us:

> "Landscape is not just there. It was here long, long before we were even dreamed. It was here without us. It watched us arrive."
>
> —Dr. John O'Donoghue,
> "Stone as the Tabernacle of Memory"

Indeed. John O' has captured my interest, and he certainly makes a better case for this place than did Conqueror Ludlow.

Jana Zvibleman

Vast

Outside, at first glance, The Burren is unimpressive. Limestone, limestone, and limestone, as grayish-white as our home skies. Plus a few other rocks, black and gray, all exposed on hundreds of square miles.

As we pick our way over cracks and crevices, we discuss how difficult it is to fathom: millions of years ago, the ocean was right here. I look toward the far horizon and realize vastness.

And look, a *cairn*! Someone has piled rocks one on another. And here are more—a stack of only two; seven; three. A tower of many, high as my knee; another high as my elbow.

Bruce and I first came upon such elementary sculptures on an uphill path leading to a Buddhist shrine, in Massachusetts of all place. Ever since, we've been aficionados and builders. Buddhists and Celts and we Jewish Yanks.

Here stand bevies of *cairns*, I'm guessing built by every tourist since ol' Ludlow. We maneuver amidst clusters of *cairns*, taking care to not be the cause of a topple. Inevitably, we each squat and select untouched stones with flat sides; we concentrate, adding our signatures to this public playground.

Then we meander farther, and oh! A blossom, in this impossible terrain. And another. *These* have thick-leaves and tiny, deeply red petals. *This* is delicate, pale. "Look over *here*." And more, of diverse colors, shapes, sizes. We are surprised to recognize several flowers, cousins to those in our very backyard. We recite names: helleborine, vetch, thistle, heather. St. John's wort. Thyme. Orchids, and orchids too, but different. Who knows, we may even be right.

It's not till afterwards we read with better attention

and learn how unusual it is that Arctic, Alpine, and Mediterranean plants dwell here as neighbors. Plus: rocks are *not* to be moved in the Burren. *Oops.* The book says some of the *cairns* are from early *early* times. *Hmm.* Which among that forest of stacks were *antiques*? Did we mess with history? Well, at least we weren't so crass as to pocket any as souvenirs.

I think of a child of yore clattering those rocks together. An *ancient toddler*; that phrase fascinates me. Watching his grandmother as she gauges sizes, slowly selects, positions one stone on another. The child trying out his prehensile grasp, and with repetition, mastering it. We definitely should add *cairn*-building as an activity in Montessori classrooms. I imagine those long-ago humans as entranced as are Bruce and I by this interaction with the earth. Making a mark, meditatively, respectfully. None of us knowing whether our *cairn* would last for eternity or be knocked over that very night by a local feral goat, fox, hare, or pine marten. An ancient woman having no notion that a woman from a distant continent, in a distant time, would pick up the very same stone, stone, stone, recreating her art.

The Ancient Cooking Place

Now riding out in the boonies, I shout, "Bruce, turn the car around! I saw a sign."

"A sign? What kind of sign?"

"A *sign*. It said Ancient Cooking Place. Sounds good."

I think of our kitchen back home. The scarred counter-tops—all two feet of them; the duct-taped knobs on the erratic oven; the flimsy cabinet doors; shelves lined with peeling Contact Paper. Ancient? We're talking *1960s*.

Because we chose to purchase tickets to Ireland, a modernization of our kitchen will remain on the back burner, until the quarters in the Quaker Oats can replenish themselves. So, maybe it'll make us feel better to check out an even older and *more* rustic Cooking Place.

We remember nothing in the guidebooks about such a site, so we have no idea who did their cooking here. We park and start on foot along a path lined by stone walls. The sea is within our view, and this area seems a nice enough venue for the culinary arts. We proceed.

The wildflowers are lovely.

Now we're passing a van, which is thwacked, rusted, so entrenched in weedy grasses it's likely been parked here since before Adam and Eve covered their privates with shamrocks. Boxes, both wooden and cardboard, intact and battered, are scattered around, plus an assortment of partial chairs and crooked stools, wheels and bottles, hand tools, pots, and unidentifiable artifacts. The lived-in look. We whisper to each other that this is probably home to a family of today's version of Irish *travellers*. ("Tinkers"? We're ignorant, yet pretty sure "gypsies" is a derogatory term) Anyway, this might be one vehicle of a modern caravan. Oh, it dawns on me, *caravan* must be where the word *van* comes from.

Anyway, this is old, but not *olden*—right? We keep on the path.

And on.

On each side spread pastures and fields. We pass a horse and her foal of a different color. Six huge white cows, or are they bulls? We're still on the splendid, charactered country path, and look, poppies, brilliant red. The day is grand.

But that so-called Place?

As we walk, we hold hands, which is one of my life's pleasures, so I can't complain.

And now llamas with their skinny-necked llama babies, whose enormous eyes ponder us. And further along, disinterested sheep. The livestock is useless in providing directions.

When we left our car, we didn't prepare for a long hike. We did grab camera and binoculars, and they're getting heavy. We're thirsty.

Bruce gives me his intimate gesture of reassurance: three gentle, quick squeezes to my hand.

Now we're relieved to spot, way up ahead, a human figure with a canine one, growing larger as they move toward us. When they're close enough for us to discern the wool cap and comfy jacket on the human, and the tongue on the dog, we exchange greetings and then inquire about the Cooking Place.

"Ah, that. Yeh've passed it, yeh have. It's back that a-way, and through the gate." He gestures vaguely behind us and toward the Atlantic Ocean.

Oh.

We turn to face from whence we came. Now the man and dog are ahead of us. Now they're gone.

Or were they ever there?

Do you remember a gate? *I don't remember a gate.*

We trudge back and back, and are no less thirsty. Hello again, sheep. Hi, llamas, remember us? Still no gate. Howdy bulls—or are you cows?

One of Bruce's standard phrases rings out, "I have a solution!" To me, it appears like a comic speech bubble above his head, accompanied by a lightbulb. I'm always amazed at his success at jerry-rigging the way through a dilemma. *When* he's successful. Now his idea is *the heck with a gate*, and it's over that rock wall we go.

Well. Here are high grasses, and rocks, and more walking, and more walls, and we come up with several choice suggestions for the Republic of Ireland's Department of Signage. A fence or two, more rocks, more climbing over.

After what the Irish would call a donkey's age, I declare, "Forget it"; Bruce advocates for persevering.

Eventually he says, "This is ridiculous." *I* am sure we must be just about there. The give-up urge is compelling, yet the push-on momentum keeps winning. We *are* getting closer to the sea, a pleasing prospect. Sure would like to get a look at this *feckin'* kitchen already, just for the point of it. We wouldn't mind a taste, too, of whatever's in the oven.

Someone certainly had a long way to carry their grocery bags.

Another wall or two.

Now no grasses; it's rock only underfoot, the flat limestone of The Burren.

We come to large stones, wider than that van, taller than two of me. Several groupings of these rocks define slight curves. Is this it? No information in any language, no ticket taker, no don't-touch warning. No pit. No blackened marks from fires. No bones nor carrot peels lying about.

Imagination is our guide here. Let's *pretend* this is the Place. The place of stewing and simmering, long before Julia Child was knee-high to a stick of butter.

I huddle against the concave side of the largest rock grouping and try to conjure up the image of a woman tending a fire. Roasting fish? Boiling dried grasses?

I *don't* decide to inquire next time we're at a visitor information bureau — the *facts* aren't what I'm wanting. I am sensing a strange inner pull; I wonder if I'm being touched by some primordial sisterly spirit. I reach back through memories of myself a mere twenty-five years ago: In the 1970s I was young "earth-mother," grinding whole-wheat berries into flour and kneading heavy dough, stirring thick whole-grain-and-bean soup in my black cast-iron pot. Domestic labor throughout the day, after day after day, fiercely intent on nourishing the little ones who slumbered on my back, watched from my hip, clutched my knees. I remember the aches in my back, arms, feet. My emotions, from contentment to boredom, fulfillment to despair. Now those memories are throbbing into a visceral sensation, a communal touch with the woman, women, who once tended *this* hearth.

My ancient sister, cooking right here, would occasionally have lifted her gaze up from her work, to the sea. During my days spent within my kitchen, I looked out the window at an asphalt driveway and a fence. *She* probably squatted next to her grandmother, aunts, nieces; maybe they sang together. I stood alone, only occasionally propping the phone receiver chin-to-shoulder and stretching the cord across the room to the sink, hearing the voice of an unseen friend while I rinsed brown rice. When I felt lonely during those hours, which was often, I longed to be in the presence of what I fantasized as "my tribe."

I think not only of the difference but also of the commonalities of our experiences, me and my kinswomen of yore. We're all grinding, chopping, kneading, stirring, tasting, serving.

"Hey where'd you go? Here's a very cool shot!" It's Bruce, here and now, coming around a rock, gesturing to me to stand by a shallow pool in the stones, where he photographs my reflection.

After sharing my inner reflections, we trek back on rock, through grasses, over walls, past wildflowers, to appreciate our plastic water bottles and packaged protein bars.

Thickly Settled

We've loved the small towns' pink and yellow and blue storefronts, the flower boxes and shutters on cottages. The Burren's blossoms, the sea vistas, the mind-boggling monuments in cow pastures, the llama eyes. Rural Ireland has charmed our woolen socks off. Now we're eager for city culture and have arranged to meet up again with Catherine, who's traveled to Dublin. Moving meter-by-meter closer toward civilization, we puzzle at several signs proclaiming Thickly Settled. Eventually, we seem to roll over some invisible line: coincidence or not, dark clouds gather overhead, and the heavens open with a downpour, just as we're closed in by traffic, buildings, and tossed cigarette butts.

Though hungry for dinner, we need to first find a home base. Following the guidebook and ringing doorbells, we discover the B&Bs are occupied, the recommended hotel is woeful, the youth hostel is cramped and smelly, and we're *knackered*. We consider driving right back to somewhere, anywhere, in the countryside. We both groan at the thought of additional car time.

A few more roundabouts, and we see storefronts that seem to promise discoveries, and a park with, oh, swans. There's a theater. We make several bonus right-hand turns, pull into a parking spot, and now we're perched on yet another doorstep, asking for room at the inn.

This icebox-shaped proprietress has a scowl that plunges down into my bones. She presses her fists against her hips. And nods.

As we enter her domain and lug our luggage—ah, no wonder they call it that—behind her bulk, up creaking stairs, she's muttering, "Terrible weather, what a terrible rainy day, a terrible, terrible day of terrible weather."

On the wall hangs a poster confiding, "If it was raining soup, the Irish would go out with forks," attributed to Brendan Behan.

On the landing, *herself* is fiddling with the ornate relic door key, and I'm mentally adding *terrible* to my essential Irish vocabulary list, when she adds, "Oh, but I'm not complaining, don't get me wrong."

Hats to Let

We're on the streets of Dublin with Catherine and Fiona, window shopping. In one display, hats. Ladies' hats. Ladies' wondrous hats. I pull my two ladies with me, in through the door of my very first millinery.

Floor-to-ceiling shelves of red, mauve, lavender, and gray hats. Hot pink hats and powder blue hats. Veiled hats and plumed hats. Flowered hats and laced hats. Fancy hats and fancier hats.

The shop is brim full. *Chapeaus* with full brims. Brims that brim out, and brims that brim out farther, and brims that spread practically from one wall to the other. Circumferences that could swoop from here to America— though Americans wouldn't know what to do with such hats.

One whole wall in the shop is a mirror. As the three of us place one and then another piece of elegance on our heads, we view the transformation of our total beings.

Under a soft-yellow, floppy-brimmed creation, I become a Madam, strolling through manicured spring gardens. I try on a tailored mauve number, and I am poised in a reception line offering my delicately gloved hand to a Duke.

Catherine, next to me in the mirror, is posture-perfect under what looks like the skirt of a ballgown: an aubergine-colored, asymmetrical number, topped by a lacey floral swish, makes her Queen Mother. Under feathers and pinky ribbons is Princess Fiona, the Maid of Giggles.

This one after that one, the head-fashions transport us to their worlds of formal teas and gracious introductions, while our little *Colleen* makes silly faces. Ballrooms and cordials, and she's dancing in circles. We conceal blushes while accepting clandestine compliments; our whispered *tête-à-têtes* are punctuated by her squeals. We're hearing the violinist bow a waltz, while at our feet Fiona somersaults clumsily.

Up marches the shop proprietress. She is buxom, tailored, and suspiciously bare-headed. Her mauve lipstick rises only at the very corners. "May I show you anything to *let* or *purchase*, then?"

I bare my head, stiffen my back, and reply, "No, really. None of these will do."

"Thank you, *luv*, no," Catherine says. She adds, "Sorry, but our upcoming royal engagement requires *high* fashion, with *tasteful* garnishes." (Well, she doesn't add that, but I'm wishing she would.)

Back outside the window, all three of us giggle. I recite the dialogue between two upright poodles in the children's book, *Go Dog Go*:

"Hello."

"Hello."

"Do you like my hat?"

"No I do not like your hat."

"Goodbye."

"Goodbye."

To Market

We come upon Moore Street. Bruce and I exclaim, "*Agnes Brown's* place!" We relished the book *The Mammy* by Brendon O'Carrol, plus its sequels, *The Chiselers* and *The Granny*. We were especially fond of the heroine Agnes, who bore her poverty and the related woes of dear old Ireland with spunk, in a manner much different than that of pitiful Angela of *Angela's Ashes* fame.

So I'm eager to stride into the very location where the Mammy toiled as a fruit vendor. Her professional and social domain was a rustic booth crammed among others in the hustle and bustle of *this* actual marketplace.

Bruce decides for his own reasons—the sound of fiddling from the other direction—not to enter this market. Catherine is game. As she and I stride on the cobblestones, stepping around browned apples, cigarette butts, miscellaneous peels, unidentified mush, she says, "Yeah, this litter is a given." I'm paying more attention to the mélange of aromas: bread, flowers, produce, and people, some fresh, some rotting.

We approach a counter of wooden planks covered by heaps of fruit. Yellows, reds, oranges. Behind them stands a towering woman with an angular, yellowed face and hook nose. Black scraggly curls stick out around a frayed yellow paisley headscarf. Padding her skinny body are layers upon layers of tattered clothing, some orange, some brown; flowered, plaid, dotted.

I contemplate her, while she hollers in a deep voice, "Get pro-duce here. Get it! Won't last all day. Get yer fruit!" She looks familiar.

Topping her outfit is a faded blue gingham apron, with a long pocket across her midsection. "That pocket's where the money is kept," Catherine tells me in a low voice. "The larger notes, they keep down their bras, in a sock. But, yeh see, nobody would dare to pickpocket any of the Moore Street traders. They're like the Mafia—you'd never make it out of the street alive."

The woman glares at us through slits of dark eyes; a burning cigarette dangles from her mouth. She looks tougher than any thug in gangster movies.

Scared or not, I *must* buy something from The Mammy.

I step closer to her display and see open brown paper bags of purple orbs. I reach into one bag and palm three plums; they're soft enough to be eaten today. As I stick out my selection toward the woman, her hoarse voice blasts, "Can't weigh the plums, *luv!*"

I can't remember ever being called *luv* before, and I've certainly never heard the word nor the concept thus pummeled.

She repeats, "Can't. Weigh. The. Plums."

I freeze.

I'm not supposed to *weigh* them? Hey, I'm not. Maybe she means *she* can't be bothered, that customers are supposed to weigh the fruit *themselves*? I look around. No scale. Also, no Catherine.

"I, *um,* want these, please," I say.

"CAN'T WEIGH THE PLUMS, *LUV.*"

"Oh. Uh, how much are they?"

She grabs up a full bag, points at a hand-scrawled tag, and declares, "A pound for a pound."

I want to appease Missus Toughlove. But I have no idea how much the bag weighs. Plus, my mind is incapable of language translation, let alone monetary mathematical conversion, especially under such duress.

What am I supposed to do? May as well make a guess. After all, faking it is one strategy I've used around authority figures much of my life, from kindergarten with Mrs. Duffy to offices with *good ol' boy* bosses. Maybe this will work: I pick up the bag I had raided, and I also manage to transfer a wad of *punts* from my trembling fingers to her impatient palm in its ragged fingerless glove. She grunts. So I've given the right amount? Or it's too much, and she's duped this tourist. In any case her chin raises and makes a slight move to the right. I surmise me and my plums are now dismissed; my knees are weak with relief.

Now, Catherine has reappeared holding bananas, and the woman's glare turns to her, declaring, "Don't break the bananas! They're NOT in-di-vidual."

Escaping back through the maze of Moore Street, I'm begrudging the woman neither the emotion nor the money, since I'm remembering Agnes' hardships in her widowhood, with all those mouths to feed, and a pubescent son fretting about "me Willy." (You'll have to read the book yourself for that hilarious reference.) Anyway, now that we're at a safe distance, Catherine and I are releasing our tensions through uncontrollable giggles. A survivor of Irish Catholic schooling, she gasps, "I feel like I've been told off again by a nun." She shivers, then rants, "The feckin' vendor was totally uninterested in the needs and wants of these two very obvious *blow-ins*."

Soon we're telling our tale to Bruce, or rather *tales*, because I'm saying, "This woman was skinny as a chopstick," and Catherine is saying "She was as wide as she was tall," and I'm saying, "She was *very* tall," and Catherine is saying "The tyrant was shorter than a bug, but they stand behind their stalls on upturned milk crates."

We do concur that we had indeed visited the world of *The Mammy*, and we each slurp a plum.

Jana Zvibleman

Pub Talk, a Sequel

Bruce and I learned early-on from Rory: drinking is not only what many Irish *do*, it's also the essential subject of their soliloquies. That cliché about Eskimos having many names for snow? The Irish cup runneth over with words for drunk, including but not limited to: *locked, mouldy, ossified, polluted, twisted, langers, buckled, blutered, legless, flutered, baloobas, jarred,* and *rotten.*

I don't know whether there are subtle differences in meaning; subtleties don't seem to go along with—here's another—*being on the gargle.*

Now two young men, who I guess have been sitting here at McGans for half their lives, are philosophizing about the true national sport.

One slurs out, "The vodka drunk is a body drunk. The Guinness drunk is a mind drunk."

The next time I look at this pair, they've thrown their arms around each others' shoulders, that so-called "Christian side hug." One declares "When I say 'I love you,' it means . . ." (Darn, I can't understand the mumbled revelation.)

The other responds, "If I say 'I love you,' it means . . ." (Again, too garbled for me to learn the essence of their devotion.) They both have droopy eyes and well-satisfied smiles. I imagine them coming to fisticuffs before this night is out.

Yer Man

At the beginning of our travels, whenever we are out and about in a town and need to *go*, we don't have to hold it long. There's a pub nearby. Just scoot in and venture down its dark back hallway. The posters pointing to Toilet lead us along the trail of all those Guinness guzzlers who frequently and woozily stumble to what they call *the jacks*. Yet, through odiferous trials and stinky tribulations, we become reluctant. At long last, Catherine clues us in: "Argh! *Not* the pubs! Get to a hotel. *They're* clean."

So, in Dublin, here I go, into not a common pub but instead the grand entryway of a hospitality establishment.To appear not the *blow-in* I am, I stride through the lobby, acting at home around its plush couches and deep leather chairs, polished end tables, elegant lamps, spotless mirrors. I'm going for a demeanor of *privileged*, as if I lease a suite here regularly when I touch in from my Madagascarian safari, Indonesian grand tour, or tea with Her Majesty. At the far end of the lobby, I'm making a big show of appreciating the satiny wallpaper plus the reproductions of masterpieces hanging over it. Now I look up at the gilded clock, glance at my (bare) wrist just for good measure, shake my head with a smile as if bemused by my ever-tardy tryst companion, then continue to amble, scrutinizing one landscape after another. My script says to appear as if I would be content to grow aged and expire right here on this carpet. Coming to a corner, I turn. Now I *charge*, praying, praying this is the hallway to the lavatory. Yes! Now I'm pulling open the door, stepping right in and—*yer man*, whoever he may be, stands there relieving himself.

He's looking up and stammering "Sorry," and I'm backing out and belatedly seeing the clue on this door, which tells me *FIR* and not *MNÅ* in plain Celtic, and quick I'm turning and am retracing my route, glancing neither left nor right, and I'm out on the street and through gritted teeth telling Bruce we need to get to a feckin' different hotel, or I don't care even a pub, *like now.*

The Drama of It All

L ooking at the faces and hair, listening to the chitter-
chatter, we're pleased to be the only foreigners in the
theatre for *The Chastitute* by celebrated playwright John B.
Keane, of whom we have no inkling. The playbill lauds him
as "king of the one-liner, [his]ear finely tuned to the lilts
and nuances of his native Kerry people's speak."

We're lucky, we are, to get a ticket, we're told by the
ticket-seller: this masterpiece has been sold out through
its run, it has, and is held over due to popular demand, it is.

So what might *chastitute* mean? Once the curtain is
raised, we verify it's rather what it sounds like: the opposite
of a prostitute. The limelight is on John Bosco McLaine,
who stays chaste not by choice. In fact, lust drives him to
distraction, which is drink. Each time he does find himself
in the throes of carnal opportunity, he falls out of bed or is
in some other way halted, by his guilt. His *conscience* itself
is depicted on center stage by two arguing heads situated
on a box. The head that holds my attention is the epitome
of *dour*, with whitened face and blackened lips, ranting hell
and brimstone.

John's resistance to hanky-panky, and giving-in to
hanky-panky, and remorse about hanky-panky, all lead
him back to the pint. All the men and women around us,
as one, moan deeply with our hero's agonies.

The play is ruthless in its derision of The Church; the
audience response builds from chuckles to loud celebra-
tory hoots. I find this fascinating. Do they habitually dep-
recate their religion Monday through Saturday, then kneel
humbly at Sunday mass? Could laughter at the expense
of priests serve to cleanse the soul? Is confession really a

punchline? Seems to me the derision might be considered blasphemous and might induce further guilt. But what do I know of Catholicism.

At intermission, we're shouldered upstairs with the crowd to the theatre bar, where most queue up for Guiness, save the few outliers who choose coffee, probably enhanced with shots of Jameson. For me, more than enough stimulus is provided by the up-close-and-personal aromas of flowery perfume, spicy cologne, dumpster breath, cigarette smoke, and booze. The lights flicker, people gulp their dregs, and we're seated again to watch John imbibing even more. At the end, our hero says *phooey* to The Church, decides *not* to use a gun to blow his own brains out, and (spoiler alert) marks the occasion with booze.

We join the Irish populace bounding up for a rousing ovation.

Johnny B.

Throughout Dublin, brochures tout The Angela's Ashes Tour. We both had teared up through the popular book, but neither of us feels any inclination to gawk at the hovel where Frank McCourt starved, nor the school where he was thrashed—superb writer though he is.

We do make our way to Dublin's Abbey Theatre, the *famed* Abbey Theater, renowned worldwide, unknown to us. There we attend another apparently classic play, *Big Maggie*, also by John B. Keane. The heroine was once a proper wife to a philandering drunk, a good mother to ungrateful children; now her hubby is dead and children grown. The play is set in the late 1960s when women's sad lot was beginning to change. Without labeling herself a feminist, Maggie shoves out of the old mold. Armed with her mouth, she confronts the world, daring to be hard, selfish, adventurous, biting, and risqué. The audience *hurrahs*.

Later, we tell Catherine's parents about our theatregoing. Her father Alfie says, "Ah yes, Johnny B. it is, I went to school with him." Later still, a Bed & Breakfast hostess says, "Oh, sure, sure, John Keane, we all know him. He's from my town, a'course."

Lifting

We visit Parnell Square, and within it the Garden of Remembrance, apparently once grand but today weedy and worn. We happen upon a larger-than-life metal statue. Sculpted swans; human boys and girls. Ah, The Children of Lir! We gaze up at the poor waifs who have hunched shoulders and closed eyes; they're drooping and dropped, heads down. Yet the artist has made this static sculpture a dynamic story: one child is lifting his arms, and you can see they're all transforming into four great birds rising higher together, spreading their new wings, becoming a protected species.

Under their tragedy and triumph, we settle on concrete and eat our vegetarian sandwiches.

Illuminated

We've been told to see *The Book of Kells*, an illuminated Latin manuscript containing the Gospels of the New Testament, created by monks.

Monks, New Testament, Gospels, Latin—*naw*, thanks.

Oh well, here we are by Trinity College, so let's have a peek.

First, the gift shop. I find a sterilized quill feather in a labeled plastic package. This feather is dyed blue; affixed to its tip is a shiny gold-colored pen nib. I buy it, with regret that I discarded my find of that raw, authentic quill feather back among the live swans.

Now the big-deal Kells feature: Locked in glass cases, books larger than a pope's headdress sit opened. We jostle among other tourists to have a look. The pages are covered with elaborate illustrations, swirling decorations, ornate text. Mythical beasts, Celtic knots, crosses and other Christian symbolism, in rich golds, vibrant maroons, purples.

Okay, nice. Let's go find something to eat.

Where to Get Off

B ruce and I go for a wee bit of time to the town of Leixlip, which means "salmon run," then to travel back to Dublin we board a bright red double-decker public bus. We climb the steep metal stairs, firmly holding onto both handrails, and nab the seats in the very front, where we settle to look out the picture window. It's a kick to ride directly over the driver, enjoying a tourist-bird's-eye view of the bustling streets.

We pass Phoenix Park, said to be home to not a phoenix but the King's red deer. They would be fun to see. Coke-bottle red, or Irish-hair red? Why deer in an urban park? Does the king alone—what king?— claim the privilege of shooting arrows into them? We glimpse topiary but no creatures.

When my navigator deems we're close to our destination, we balance our way back down the steps while the bus jostles, and we stumble toward the driver. Bruce asks, "Am I right that O'Connell Street is coming up in two stops?"

A woman in the nearby seat calls out, "Yeh've a long way to go before O'Connell Street! Ah, *luv*, yeh'd better sit down here."

"Thanks, that's okay," Bruce says. He stands in front of me, his back braced against the same pole I cling to.

"Yeh'd best sit down right here," the woman insists, moving her bulging bags, scooting over a bit, and patting the space next to her. "Yeh've a long way to O'Connell Street! I know. Sit right here."

He looks toward me, I nod, and he moves toward the seat. Now she notices me.

"Ah," she says, jumping to her feet, "An' your wife can sit here too. Yeh need her to tell yeh where to get off!"

As Bruce sits, she shuffles forward a couple of steps. With her face almost kissing distance from mine, I smell a bit of the whiskey on her breath.

Wanting to return her friendliness, I say the first thing that jostles into my mind. "Yeah, I'm always telling him where to *get off.*"

We trade positions, bumping shoulders, her chuckling, "Ah, yes, it's familiar, I know what you mean! I'm telling my hubby the same!"

Half-Eleven

We're walking up to the bus stop at Wellington Quay, watching for the 23:30. That's "half-eleven" p.m. Which is eleven-thirty p.m. I'll get the hang of this yet.

We hear singing. How lovely. What language is that? A group of people are harmonizing: two young women, one young man, a woman and man probably in their fifties. All dark haired, dark skinned. Pakistani, I guess, based on nothing.

A red-haired, pale-skinned woman joins them, the singing ends, and they're laughing and talking. I say, "That was so nice! Please sing more," and one laughs and translates to the others. Now they do start singing again. It's in English, a song I know and *so* did not expect. "When Israel was in Egypt land/Let my people go!" I join in on the Passover song, though their tune is slightly different than the one I'm familiar with. Then a pause with more talking and laughing among them, and they sing a song I do not *get*. Oh, it's in Spanish. Are they Ecuadorian? But we've been in that country, and the pronunciation there was much easier for us to understand.

"Spaniards," Bruce says. "I can tell by the dialect."

Next is "Swing Low Sweet Chariot," in Spanish.

A man says in English, "We take requests," but Bruce and I don't come up with anything, and no one else seems to be listening, so they sing another lively new-to-us song. A bus arrives; some of them board, bidding *adios* to the others.

"Where are you from?" I ask.

"Spain. The Basque region."

Smiles and thanks and waves, and we travelers all part, to our separate worlds.

Knot

The Celtic knot is ubiquitous, decorating pub doors, dog collars, carpets, earrings. In my notebook, my pen wanders away from words and attempts to draw the infinitely coiling design, lines winding back upon themselves, curving into puzzles of symmetry. I'm clumsy at it. How do they bring a timeless destination around to merge with the beginning of beginnings?

After days of seeing the knot and hours attempting to recreate it, I sense it gradually enter my being. Loop around, north, loop around, west, loop around, south....*Getting* this symbol becomes an attempt to attune with the natives on some subliminal level. Though, I'll bet your average Connor and Cara would tangle up trying to draw a Celtic knot. Or, maybe in school they're drilled to execute perfect knots, which I imagine would bore the awe right out of children.

The logo of the Dublin bus line features what I see as an aborted version of the classic Celtic knot, adapted to suggest a transportation route. Topped by a turret-y thing. On the buses, it's clever though not intriguing at all; I imagine it on a flip chart, being officially approved by executives of the corporation's marketing division.

Jana Zvibleman

I First Laid My Eyes On

Downtown Dublin. Now, who am I to criticize the Pope's policy on birth control? But may I merely suggest it just might be related to the shoulder-to-shoulder throngs here? Plus, I wonder whether the Catholic multitudes have anything to do with the Church calling its services "mass."

We make our way to O'Connell Street, where we pay our proper gawking respects to the bullet holes in the huge, noble monuments depicting leaders of the fight for independence, some flanked by angels with wreaths on their heads, enormous wings, and round shields. I'm most impressed by a leader who is female, a proud heroine who was shot not only in the arm but also, ouch, in the breast— or at least that looks to be the fate of her graven image. We read plaques, such as: "This is where, in 1916, the whole building was bombed . . . the columns remained, but . . .." I've not been motivated to a deep study of the upheaval, yet I do commiserate with all who suffered during the Troubles. I can bet Bruce is singing in his head, "Everybody's got troubles, troubles, troubles/ nobody's satisfied." Words so often trigger songs from him, leaving other people puzzled by his seeming non-sequiturs. But he stays silent here; he wouldn't make light of these grave memories.

We wander down this street, then this one, merging with everyday Irish folk. A bevy of teen girls in short-skirted school uniforms. A couple holding hands, wearing matching hairstyles, leather jackets, and bluejeans; maybe they're the same gender, maybe not. A wobbling senior pulling a wheeled shopping cart. Young men stumbling out of pubs, knocking against each other, howling.

Now we come upon a monument to such commoners

themselves. It's two women sharing a bench: a worn-looking older matron plus a young prim lady, life-sized and bronzed. One of the metal shopping bags at their feet bears the logo of a nearby department store (smart product placement); the other bag is currently being sat upon by two in-the-flesh children.

I'm scanning the guidebook to read about this bench statue when I notice the words Grafton Street. "Oh, look, look! We're near the statue of *Molly Malone*. Molly Malone!"

I must digress to explain, my grade-school public education was dense with the list of the capitals of all of our country's states (which I can no longer recite and still don't care about) and the glory of U. S. independence ("Oh say can you see?"). Also, we learned the essential details about our state, Missouri: its motto (Show Me); bird (I still have bluebird memorized, though I never saw one there), and flower (rose? dandelion?).

But any information pertaining to Ireland, a miniscule, faraway island, was sparse. Oh, we colored in leprechauns and traced shamrocks, plus heard a smattering of the wearin' of the green and the eatin' of the cabbage, once a year. But our textbooks otherwise ignored the Irish people's history, contributions, and tribulations.

Save for a song. That song we first-graders belted out, and we second graders belted out, and when we were third graders and fourth and fifth and sixth graders too, we were sure enough still sitting in our desks belting out: *In Dublin's fair city/ where girls are so pretty* . . . Yes, the timeless anthem to *sweet Molly Malone*. I've neglected her for so long, I didn't even think about arriving right on her very *streets wide and narrow*.

Dublin it is, right under our feet and everywhere filling

our gaze. I say we must hustle through the downtown here and left at this corner and across, dodging the "look out!" oncoming double-decker, amongst people speaking in every tongue of Babel, till who do I spy rising above a gaggle of bell-bottomed teenagers slouching all around her skirts, gabbing and chewing on their sweets, but *herself*. Herself solidified, clutching her basket and looking for all the world like she'll endure, though she's sold her last *cockle*, her last *mussel* dead and gone. She's *alive, alive* no, but proud in her stance and more eternal than the nearby Irish Permanent Bank and Insurance Company. Inspired I am—even compelled and obligated—to honor her with the singing.

Now while I'm not shy, I'm not given to singing in public. I haven't even added my voice to a pub session, though I'd probably be safely oblivious, since each drinking patron keeps one ear on the fiddling while the other ear's filled with the cacophony of blarney. Yet here on the street, I must sing, and I trust no one will pay me any mind. For sure not the girls (who, despite the claim in the Molly Malone song, are not really all that *pretty*, primping their bold face paint and bottle-blacked hair). The lads are preoccupied with their posturing to impress the lasses. Anyway, they wouldn't be able hear me above their own noise demanding that Johnny or Margaret, "Watch the drippin' feckin' ice cream before it's all over the lot of us," and giggling, "Yer mate there is givin' yeh the eye," and shrieking, "Shut yer *gob*! Naw he's not, yeh *eejit*!"

I'm motivated, so I plunge into immortalizing this moment when *I first laid my eyes on sweet Molly Malone*. At last, I can let loose with the rare worthwhile lesson from all my years of grade-school confinement. (I've also acknowledged that they taught me the useful *cha-cha-cha* movement.) Molly, I believe, would soon go hoarse, cockling and musseling above this traffic and human din, day-in day-out, not to mention she'd have a hard time maneuvering her wheelbarrow through this population explosion.

I do appreciate that my dear suffering *hubby* does not try to reason me out of my debut, and that he seems to be listening. For even were I to *die of a fever*, no one could save him from my ghost's *kvetching* if he now pretended he didn't know me.

By the way, friends and acquaintances had told us not to bother with Dublin. "Give Dublin at most one day," they said. They warned how disappointing Dublin would be if we saved it till after discovering the *gorgeousness* of the west. Which, except for my serenading Molly, it is, since we did.

Commerce

We may as well fill the now-gaping spaces inside our luggage. Throughout our trip, tiny shops and bustling marketplaces are eager to oblige us.

In one, I choose a comfy handknit-I-assume cardigan cable sweater, the color of pub smoke. Labeled Blarney Woolen Mills, it's cotton and linen. My grade school (disparaged above) had led me to believe "the land of cotton" was only the American south.

Bruce finds a trim vest, which *is* woolen, dark royal blue with a grid of thin white lines. He's always been a stylin' guy, changin' with the times. During his high school years, he worked at a supermarket so he could afford a sharp wardrobe; he ironed his shirts, made sure his pants were fashionably tight, kept his naturally curly hair glued down straight and shiny. Then during our hippie days, while we disdained superficial material possessions, his attire was *right on:* in-vogue baggy, worn jeans with a red kerchief sticking out of the back pocket; plaid flannel shirt; denim jacket decorated with right-wing and Beatles buttons; thick truckin' boots; a variety of cool caps; and a small gold hoop through one earlobe. These days he dresses again, for work, in pressed shirts, and ties. This dapper vest will enhance his professional look.

Now at an open-air market, I fall in love with a wide woolen shawl that makes me feel wrapped in femininity and timeless elegance. It'll work in the Oregon rain, won't it? My new garment is pale sage green and just the right balance of lightness and heft.

Bruce buys a herringbone cap to add to his hat collection, which includes—but is not limited to—the following styles:

stingy brim, fisherman, beret, stocking, aviator. Plus too many baseball caps. And one brown suede number, lumpy and asymmetrical, officially called a "stupid hat." Oh, and his formal bowler; he dons that for our rare fancy occasion, despite my visceral revulsion. (Many a man, seeing his bowler, has been known to covet it.)

This *new* purchase is the classic slanted-with-a-front-brim fashion we know as a Jeff cap; we've heard it referred to also as a flat, newsboy, or golfer cap; the Irish vender calls it a *paddy* cap. I think the style helps even a plain man look good, and Bruce quite dashing. He acquires also a practical brimmed rain hat of dark blue, waxed duck cloth; in that too he looks *très chic* (pardon my French, but I still lack the Irish word for cute).

In every nook and cranny of every shop is Guinness paraphernalia. It holds zero interest for me, while Bruce treats himself to handfuls of the pointless items. I know it's their corniness he's after: a refrigerator magnet depicts a beaming chap hauling a cart in which squats his humongous, grinning horse; a sticker has a toucan with a pint of *the black stuff* balanced on its huge orange beak; a coaster features a policeman startled by the bulging shape of an ostrich's neck, which shows the bird has swallowed a beer glass. Such *tsotchkes* bear the slogan My Goodness My Guinness.

I am *so* tempted by dramatic-looking cloaks, hooded and down-to-the-ankle, of richly dyed soft wool. They're protective, graceful, elegant. I go so far as to try on a dark blue creation, posing in the full-length mirror, imagining myself dwelling in Medieval times, perhaps as the proprietress and mystic of a fragrant dispensary of healing herbs and incantations. I'm aware that I've not seen one damsel thus cloaked in all of our time in this country. *Hmm*, were I to wear such a wrap in our town's Bi-Mart or Payless, it may be perceived as *iffy*: mothers would hold their children close, security guards would pat me down. I take the cloak off, put it back on . . . resist the purchase. With sadness.

Claddagh rings are for sale everywhere. They feature two hands holding a heart topped by a crown. I don't know why they give me the creeps; I do note that I never see anyone wearing one.

We forgo buying the much-touted whisky and the Waterford crystalware. Yet we restock our Cadbury's chocolate stash several times and have thus done our bit to enhance the Republic's economy.

Son of Pub Talk

In every pub, the consensus seems to be *the craic is 90*, meaning a grand time is had by all. I for one continue having fun witnessing even the most mundane of interactions.

For example, a lad in a group of polluted twenty-somethings shouts, "Hold on! I dropped my wallet."

As he gropes under the table, his friend directs, "It's by yer right-hand foot! By yer right-hand foot!" The first triumphantly raises high a mostly-empty beer glass with his wallet stuck in it.

They both stand up and bow to take their leave of the three young women near them. One lad says, "Lovely, yeah, lovely to meet yeh."

The other tips his cap, saying, "I hope that yer children will be very successful."

No Such Ting

For us, the sacred sites have a strong draw—churches excepted. We've acquired a specialty map that locates the standing stones and the portal tombs, and we seek them. The Republic of Ireland is home to 187 stone circles, with the majority in County Cork.

The standing stones are, I'd stupidly say, Ireland's version of England's Stonehenge. Any resource will do a better job than I can of discussing *who* may have put them there, *what* they are, *where* they came from, and *when* and *how* they may have been constructed. The essential question for me is *why*. Why would people have spent so much effort on seemingly non-utilitarian structures? I've long been fascinated with humanity's common desire to make sense of the universe's mysteries, yearning for spiritual connection, and ingenuity in creating art about the big questions.

One afternoon we find ourselves, according to the map, not far from a town which holds another standing stone, so we head there. We find nary a hint of a monolith. In a small shop that is home to a herd of gorgeous wool sweaters, caps, and capes, we ask the proprietress for directions to the feature of interest.

"Standing stone?" She mouths the words as if they're of another language and looks at us blankly. "No. We haven't any around here."

"Well it shows on this map . . .."

She won't look at it. "I know of no such *ting*. Lived here all my life, I have. Sorry, no such *ting*."

The woman standing by the counter who was chatting with her now nods, echoing in a shrill voice, "No such *ting*. All my life." They lock eyes, raising their penciled eyebrows.

Thank you, and goodbye. We exit and more carefully scan the hill across the street: trees, cows, and grasses. Yet now we spy *something* over there, a stone's throw from the shop. We stride closer to see one upright black rock, as tall as a cow standing on its hind legs, sticking out like an aged sore thumb. Bingo.

Now, in addition to pondering the secrets of the stone itself, we wonder why the modern Irish just let it be, out bare and unguarded in a field. No fence, no ticket-taker. I can't imagine the U.S. *not* constructing boundaries for, say, Old Faithful, *not* designating off-limit areas at the Grand Canyon, *not* requiring security screening to visit the Statue of Liberty. Yet come to think of it, here the lack of hints and the denial of the townspeople may suffice as deterrents against most foreign vandals.

We are privileged to visit two of the 200 or so *portal tombs* in this country. Also called *dolmens*, which comes from the words for "table" and "stone," each has a massive capstone balanced at an angle on top of two or more huge upright stones of different heights. We are impressed and mystified by them. Such a showy way to mark entrances to burial chambers, they invite contemplation about how they were built without modern jackhammers, cranes, and zoning permits.

I can't help seeing the portal tombs as the Hebrew symbol for the word *chai*, which means "life." I grew up familiar with the *chai* decorating Jewish jewelry and note-cards, and the toast "L'Chaim": to life! Even though the *chai's* top stroke is not always angled, and it is preceded by an accent-like mark which the dolmen lacks, I put stock in the fact that these symbols, each associated with life and death, look so similar. Perhaps some expert has researched the connection, or it could be mere coincidence. In other cultures, chai means tea; dolman is an article of clothing. In any case, portal tombs elicit awe.

Hen Is It?

One afternoon, Bruce returns from some solo venture and tells me he saw a chicken out on the street. "A huge chicken. Taller than you. *Really.*"

I know he never drinks *that* much Guinness, so I reply simply, "Okay."

"Yeah, this woman was dressed as a chicken, all in feathers and a beak."

Later that night, in a pub, one cluster of young men is louder than the rest of the crowd and particularly buoyant. I ask the rowdy standing nearest me what's got them so riled up.

"He's getting married," he shouts, throwing his arm around another's shoulder. "We're having the stag party."

"Tomorrow is he marrying, then?" I ask, nonchalantly slipping into my Irish phrasing.

"Oh, no! Not for two weeks."

"Do you live here?"

"No! Not here. We're from up the road, eighteen miles."

"So do you come here all the time?"

"Oh no, never. He's getting married. It's the stag party."

"What about the women? Do the bride and her maids party too, before a wedding?"

"Yes, there are several hen parties."

"Oh, *hen* is it?" I say, never having heard that before. "*Hmmm.* My husband said he saw a woman all in feathers today."

"Yes, that would be her. They're having the hen party."

(Later, Catherine tells us "hen" probably refers to the bride about to become a wife who will "hen-peck" her hubby. Unfortunate sexism. Our further research reveals "hen" to be an old reference to the female of any species, "stag" to any male. So, fowl and deer—cross-species mating is condoned, here in this Catholic land.

Outstanding Stones

We find another stone circle and amble around its perimeter. I'm trying to sense the scene thousands of years ago, with mind-altered revelers, pensive pilgrims, surprised wanderers. On this very ground, one century after another after another, individuals would have had countless thoughts, countless views and feelings here.

In contrast to many of us here at this moment, those of old never watched a documentary about this World Heritage Property nor romped through it on a video game. *They* did not spread a polyester tablecloth near it and munch pretzels and bottled beer. *They* would not have snapped family photos in front of this cool backdrop, for next year's Christmas cards. Our contemporaries are doing such, as well as inquiring about a restroom, occupying toddlers with Legos and juice boxes, arguing about tonight's hotel accommodations.

One man, oblivious to the lot of us, concentrates on his poster-sized canvas balanced on an easel. He has pencil-sketched the stones and is now brushing on oil paints. We select a spot a respectful distance behind him, so we can observe his painting while we attempt our own. How to capture with crayons the awesomeness of this place, ordinary as grass and rocks, transcendent as human aspirations.

Maura and Alfie

To introduce Catherine's parents Maura and Alfie, I must digress to just a couple of years before. Lester was *wee* when Catherine and Rory migrated to America, six when his sister Fiona was born.

For the auspicious occasion of their grandson's first communion, Maura and Alfie had made their premier trip to the States. Catherine and Rory invited their American friends and colleagues for a home celebration after the church service. Catherine later told us the story of what led up to that:

The day before, as Maura had helped Catherine prepare a few dishes, Maura grew increasingly anxious. Come evening, she said to her daughter, "Well we'd certainly better get busy in the kitchen more; it's getting late, it is."

"Really, we've made more than enough, Mother," Catherine said.

"And forty people coming for dinner! Why, the little we've prepared? Enough? This won't feed them properly at all, at all. Oh, I am on tenterhooks, I am."

"Ah, Mother, we're all right," Catherine assured her. "It's a potluck we're having."

"Sorry? *Potluck*, is it? And what might *potluck* be?"

"It's what you do in America, Mother. Everyone will bring something."

Well, Maura couldn't grasp the notion. She slept fitfully that night for fretting that her Catherine was about to humiliate the family. She hadn't brought up her only daughter to be a bad hostess, here in this foreign land of all places, and *at that* on the occasion of dear Lester's auspicious blessing.

It was Alfie's task all morning to try to calm his wife.

In the church, he saw the need to pat her hand during the praying and give her nods and winks during the sermon, and he steadied her as she rose for communion. She kept muttering, "At least more lamb in the stew."

Maura did praise the Saints at how mature dear Lester behaved, and that Fiona managed to keep her new dress mostly unwrinkled. That seemed the extent of her joy; during the photograph session, Maura's face was as pale and rough as the Burren minus its blossoms. When the family got back to the house, she hastened to the kitchen, tied on her apron, and went about again fussing with pots.

At the allotted time, Rory set his mum-in-law in the front room, where she watched as dishes, bowls, jars, and baskets paraded in through the door. Maura was wide-eyed, *gobsmacked*. Alfie then took her elbow and guided her to the table, where she gaped, aghast at fresh-baked rolls, tortilla casserole, roasted veggies, lemon cake, guacamole with chips, zucchini bread, homemade pickles, brownies, and more. She turned her eyes upwards in thanks for the miracle.

When we arrived, we were introduced to the older, shorter, somewhat frail version of Catherine, with the same curly red hair, yet thinner. Maura's greeting: "Sorry, I'm so embarrassed," and went on that each guest brought a plate bearing mounds of food, much of which they made *themselves*. "Can yeh believe it? Oh, yeh must be insulted," she said. I tried to assure her that was not the case at all. I don't think she bought it. "Truly not? Well, no one does *seem* put off."

Alfie, a lanky former redhead, traveled the room, entering chats here and chats there with, "How'd yeh like a pint of the Guinness we imported?" With a wide smile he delivered a large, dripping glass to any taker, each time topping up his own to be hospitable.

By the time Maura nibbled just a bit of three of the desserts, and had her teacup refilled, and accepted a glass of the Guinness too, she declared with a smile, "Well, I'm going to try this when I get home, I am. Imagine! Invite my friends for dinner, and tell *them* to bring the food!"

Scoop, Ladle, Pour, and Pass

So we had met Maura and Alfie out of their element; now we have arrived with Catherine on their turf, County Wicklow. We are honored to be welcomed by this older-generation, dyed-in-the-wool Irish couple.

Maura greets us at their front door, apologizing for the weather. She's cordial as she ushers us in, yet she seems more than a wee bit nervous, looking all around, straightening a picture here and turning a lamp on there, continuously smoothing the front of her crisp, bright-plaid pinafore apron over her muted-flower dress. She seats us at the dining table where Alfie greets us by filling our glasses. Their large brood has grown and moved, save their youngest son, a six-footer, sitting next to his *da*. Yet the table is long, still able to accommodate any and all of their visiting children, grandchildren, and friends.

Maura scurries from dining room to kitchen with serving platters, tureens, and pitchers, and back to the kitchen for more. At last she surveys the spread with a frown, sighs, unties her apron and sets it aside, and settles in the head seat across from Alfie. She proceeds to scoop, ladle, pour, and pass a grand abundance.

The food is all brilliant, and dinner is enhanced by warm, gracious conversation; we finish with lovely tea in splendid chinaware. With a flourish, our grinning host and hostess present a white box to Bruce and me. We open it to find two matching glass flower vases, weighty and beautifully cut, engraved, and polished; we gush sincerely. They guide us to "the Waterford collection," display cabinets chock-full of other elegant vases, plus drinking glasses and candlestick holders. Bottles and pitchers. Bowls and more vessels.

"Wow," we say eloquently, admiring the details on the only pieces we can fully view, those at the front of the crowded shelves. We comment on the obvious: "You have so many!"

"Yes, well due to the golfing, of course," says Alfie.

"The golfing?"

"Sorry, well we used to do quite a bit of golfing, you know, and Waterford is what you're given as prizes, isn't it? So over the many years, yes, you can say we've now a bit of the Waterford!"

We're impressed with the winnings and pleased with our vases. Yet despite the couple's urging, we feel no need to go tour the esteemed *manufactory* established 200 years before, House of Waterford Crystal, in—where else?—Waterford, Ireland.

I'm worried about how we'll transport this crystal intact across the ocean, until I remember that Bruce once had a summer job as a mover, and among his many skills are padding and packing.

Now Maura dons a fresh apron and refuses our help with the clearing of the table; we're sent to the front room for more visiting, more tea, more Guinness. Just before we take our leave from their home, I admire Maura and Alfie standing in front of their entry stairs, with the polished walnut banister and the sage green wallpaper on which romp rabbits, foxes, rabbits, leaves, and flowers. "Please, may I take your photo?"

"Oh, dear, sorry let me go take my apron off," Maura says, raising her hands to fuss at her hair and then reaching around to the back of her waist.

"Please, would you please remain as you are? You're a lovely vision of the perfect hostess."

On our way to the car, Catherine exclaims, "That was truly amazing. Mother letting you photograph her *in an apron*!"

Arriving Early to the Past

It's a world-renowned wonder that was wondrously unknown to us, yet our Irish friends advise we must not continue in life without visiting New Grange. Sorry they are they can tell us not a whit about it, never having been there themselves. The guidebooks inform that despite its name, it's old, very old, and assure us it's amazing. Because the books tell that to everyone else too, it's predicted we'll encounter *shite*-loads of fellow tourists, especially at this time of year. Since we haven't booked tickets already, we may or may not get in. Our only chance, we're warned, is to get there before the rush.

So Bruce and I rise crazy early, an unnatural activity in the midst of vacation. We depart in the dark from Dublin, travel northbound for an hour and a half, and in the dawn's early light, in the middle of alien-nowhere, on the south side of the River Boyne, overlooking the World Heritage Property, we manage to find *Brú na Bóinne.* One cannot go directly to the main attractions, but must check in at the Visitor Centre. On the large parking lot are only two cars. We see no other humans along a path splendid with flowering plants, picturesque stones, pleasing bridges. We come to the entry of a modern, upscale building featuring plenty of glass. The shut door has a sign informing us of the opening time, which is over two hours from now. So. We've hustled to be at the head of a non-existent queue. We settle down on the walkway, lean against the entry wall, glad for our breakfast bars and water. We feel a bit foolish, like teens waiting for a rock concert, save that we lack that kind of passion and eager anticipation, so sleepy and chilly are we.

Eventually, inspired by the wish for a bathroom, I take

a notion to approach the front door and jiggle the handle. To my surprise, it turns. I pull the door open!

Well, open doors mean opportunity, don't they? "Hey, Bruce!"

We both step gingerly into dark and silence.

"Hello? Excuse me?" "Is anyone here?"

It's a bit spooky to be doing this, but the expansive, airy lobby does not seem threatening at all. Through the dark, we easily find the restrooms.

After taking care of business, "Should we just peek in over there?"

We begin our exclusive tour of an elaborate, professional show-and-tell about the Passage Tomb. Nothing aged about this state-of-the-art museum, which includes informational text, artifacts, illustrations. Glass-encased dioramas with realistic life-size figures bring us as close as possible to scenes of 5000 years ago, the Neolithic period. Mannequin laborers are building a structure to be used, it is postulated, for worship and/or funereal and/or birthing rituals. We almost forget to apprehend being caught, as we move from room to room, staring, pointing, whispering, reading.

We learn the construction of the mound spanned several generations, without benefit of written language. That boggles me. No blueprint, no instruction manual, though the original architects and grunt workers died and the next ones had to remember the vision and which gee-gaws screwed into which. The stones themselves were somehow brought here from far distant locations. Before the invention of the wheel. On waterways by floating the stones, and on land by rolling them over felled logs. We read it was not long ago when this site was rediscovered and restored. The original symbols were carved by craftspeople of old; graffiti was added by early twentieth century *eejits*.

Most fascinating: how the structure was designed precisely so the sun enters the pitch-black chamber only once a year, at dawn on the winter solstice, for eleven minutes.

We read that a shuttle bus leaves at regularly scheduled intervals to carry ticket holders to the actual site. If only there were a ticket seller and a busdriver!

Bruce and I have viewed only a percentage of the rich offerings in this *centre*, but we decide to be prudent and pull ourselves away. Leaving no trace, we let ourselves back out of the building and re-settle on the walkway.

We endure another boring wait, grumbling about that advice to arrive here before G-d. We could have built the structure ourselves in this amount of time. After a century, several other tourists appear. A man says to us, "Ah, yeh look like yeh're waitin' for the January sales." We remain seated as couples and small family groups gather nearby, frowning at their watches. Eventually a woman in a cloud of perfume bustles up the path from the parking lot, greets us all jovially, wiggles her key in the door, and sashays in, calling back to us, "Are yeh happy enough there? The *Centre* will open in twenty minutes, *luvs*."

Down Under

The New Grange bus bumps our group of tourists past farm fields for fifteen minutes, then delivers us back thousands of years. And here we are at the huge entry stone, with the famous carving of three spirals. Our guide points to them and gives cursory information. Basically: they're spirals; there are three of them; they're interesting, aren't they?

Into the structure, then, single file. At five-two and 115 pounds, even I have to bow and squinch to move along the channel. It's so dark I cannot see Bruce and repeatedly flump against his back.

Arriving at a chamber, we modern beings overlap shoulders with each others to fit around the perimeter. We stay as silent as the "basin stone" in the center, a horizontal slab on which I imagine a dead body. Or a dying one. Or was this an inhospitable bed for birthing? Or, *oh man*, a platform for ritualized rape?

Now the minimal light is extinguished; my lids remain wide open in pure can't-see-your-own-hand black. Black pudding? After forever in this disorienting void, we all gasp:

A miraculous white beam enters that far opening and travels to us.

Again, thick silence. As our predecessors must have done on this spot, we are honoring the sun, aren't we? We're paying homage also to the human feat of bringing brilliance into our dark spaces. The ancients accomplished it with this sophisticated architecture, the moderns with the basic magic of electricity.

I'd love to linger in these depths, contemplating nature, time, spirit. I'd appreciate this quiet going on and on, while I continue to savor the genius of humans—the seekers, the thinkers, the technicians, the builders, the artists. The archeologists and anthropologists. Historians, prehistorians. Brainiacs who *understand* electricity.

Three spirals, nine months—the gestation time of humans. A symbol inferring pregnancy, birth, other female mysteries.

And as to what went on *within* the mounds: possibly, rituals for birthings and for funerals. The two juxtaposed, to aid the reincarnation of souls.

We'll never know for sure. I'm satisfied simply to wind around in these continuous, gradually widening mental curves, universal wonderings about life.

Our time of awe is switched off, with "Now we'll allow questions and answers."

Sir, I don't say, *What, please, is the meaning of the cosmos, and what is our part in it?*

Dim illumination returns, and "A reminder to not touch the walls," the guide belts out. "Exit, please."

We obediently shuffle out to the eye-attack sunlit present. We are directed to watch our step as we reenter the bus.

The Lottery

Upon our return to the Visitor Centre, I come out of my trance remembering I heard, maybe from Catherine's father Alfie, that one may actually enter the depths of New Grange at the time of the actual winter solstice—provided one wins *the lottery*. Yet there has been no such mention by our guide here, no advertisement in the brochures nor in what we saw of the museum, no hint about such a possibility. I inquire at the ticket counter.

The elderly woman attendant looks taken aback.

"Well, yes, the lottery, yes there is the lottery," she mumbles, now gazing down at her tight knuckles.

"May I enter it?"

"Well then," she says. She goes off to speak softly to another woman on duty; they both peer back towards me. Are Americans unworthy? Do they think I'd blaspheme their solstice with, what, flashbulbs, or a striptease? The attendant rummages under a far corner of the counter, lifts out something, gestures for me to move to an isolated section. She ceremoniously, as if handling the Holy Grail, sets in front of me a black, tattered, bound notebook.

She opens it to a lined page bearing ten or more names in as many different manuscripts. Marys and Williams, Brenadas and Ferguses.

"Inscribe yer name on the last line," she directs in a clipped tone. I peek at the preceding pages and see they also are filled with such names; each accompanying address is in the Republic of Ireland.

The woman drums her fingers as I print my name and address, making the USA teeny. On the next line I print Bruce's vitals.

On the *next* line, I start on our daughter's name, with the plan to add our son's. We have cousins, friends, neighbors. Through my mind flashes a dilemma: how will we handle it if one of them is chosen instead of us?

Now I'm calculating the solstice as only four months away and pondering how Bruce and I will accumulate enough quarters to get here again so soon, wondering whether the Irish government plans to kick in for the airfare . …

The woman's shadow falls on the page. "Names only of people who are present, please. People who are present."

I reluctantly cross out the illegal name, sorry to mess up the page, sorrier to be stopped from stuffing the ballot box.

She pulls the book from my hands, inspects my entry with a frown, and snips, "The winner is to be let know." She flunks the cover shut and carries our fate back to its nook.

No numbers on a scratch-it card; no balls tumbling in a rotating cage; no G-56 nor I-21 on a Bingo card. I'm left with not even a Keep This Ticket stub. I do clutch hope.

Will the clerk tie on a blindfold and run her finger down the page until the music stops? Or tap the names one-by-one, reciting *eenie meenie miney moe*? Or will she tear the notebook pages into strips, carry them to a grand castle, and at a gala ceremony will she, dressed in feathers and glitz, scramble the names in a tophat, hold it high, and let a rural king reach in and with much fanfare pick out my name?

I must leave it up to the "luck o' the Irish"—a term which, by the way, may originally have been derogatory. During the nineteenth century, many of the miners in the California gold rush were Irish immigrants, and it was implied they were finding success not because of intelligence nor skill, but based purely on luck. Another theory is that because of the recurring troubles of the Irish over the years, their "luck" may be considered all *bad*.

Were Bruce telling this story, he would add one of his beloved musical quotes, from "Born Under a Bad Sign" sung by Albert King: "If it wasn't for bad luck, you know I wouldn't have no luck at all."

No End to the Pub Talk

B ack to this century, we have another pub adventure, during which I encounter another two young men, who also mention *luck*:

"We're from up the road. I'm from Cork."

"I live in England."

"I ride horses. I jump them."

"He *trains* horses. I used to be in horses, but I had to quit. Money, not enough money in it."

I ask, "What are you doing *here*?"

"We're looking for some women, but we can't find them."

"They avoid us. I have bad luck with the women."

I say, before I can stop myself, "Oh, that's not the way to think about it. Maybe you should change your belief."

"Ah yes," he says. "When I had a girlfriend, I had to fight them all off. Then, when we broke it off, now I can't find any. I have bad vibes."

As long as he's brought up "vibes," I persist in my philosophy—what the heck. "You have to change your thinking."

"I hafta change *somethin'*!" he says.

His friend chimes in, "His underwear, I think!"

I ignore that and say, "There are women here. You can find women."

One asks me, "Do you have children?"

"Yes," I say. "They're grown."

"How old are they?"

Instead of answering, I ask back, "How old are *you*?"

"Twenty-four."

"My youngest is twenty-four."

"Boy or girl?"

"A boy.'"

"An' do you have girls?"

"Yes, she's twenty-seven. She's in Ecuador on holiday right now."

Noting their blank look, I ask, "Do you know where Ecuador is?"

"No."

I say, "It's in South America."

"I was in Florida once. Miami. For horses."

"Wherever he is, it's for horses," says the other.

"An' there was a woman involved," the first adds.

"There's *always* a woman involved, according to him."

Drawing

We park along a large road, where we can avail ourselves of a panoramic view of green. Facing away from the car, settling on the grassy slope, we rest and sup. Then we get down to business: unpacking our watercolor crayons, oil pastels, sketchbooks, pencils and brushes. I've done visual arts all my life; Bruce has tried his hand at creative photography, yet most of his artistry has been devoted to music; I find his relatively new efforts at drawing and painting to be sweet. We've loved sporadic "art dates" for a year or so, and we prepared well to indulge during this vacation (except now we realize we should have hauled along sixteen additional variations of green). We sit near enough to share the tools, and we're facing the same trees, rocks, grasses, sky, yet our focal points and results are as different as are our bodies. We *ooo* and laugh at each other's markings, draw more, *ooo* more, pack up, and move on.

Jana Zvibleman

A Ways Up

They're mentioned in the tour books, and since bygone Ireland has been on our agenda, we decide we must visit the *beehive huts* of yore. The literature tells us they are called *Clochán*, plus gives just enough information for us to *get* they have nothing to do with bees, but rather something about monks and their fondness for isolation in little stone capsules. On our route back westward, the map shows tiny icons resembling beehives, right in this vicinity. Appalled at the admission price, we figure out we can avoid depleting our travel funds if we go the *back* way; it looks like all we have to do is follow this thin line on the map, a trail from over there. Clever Americans.

First we visit a café on a high ridge and savor the glorious view: rolling hills, ocean waves, a far beach, wee bathers. We share a mixed berry tart—ah, sublime; Irish pastries do hold their own against all deprecating reviews I've given the other cuisine. We ask the waitress about the trail; she brings us to the edge of the porch and points, "Just over that way. There's a gate."

We return to our plate to lick up every tartish crumb. Invigorated, we set out eagerly by foot. Higher we go. The path disappears.

We get to a stone wall, no gate in sight. Intrepid bargain-seekers that we are, we clamber over the wall.

Trek higher.

Long-hairy sheep. These stock-still beasts seem no relation to fluffy cloud-sillies which tend to frolic on powder-blue pajamas. Thankfully, these guys don't seem to mind us, and their pellet droppings don't hinder us. Eventually I relax my fear of being rammed.

The view
   is gone.

We've watched fog come rolling over the sea and right up the cliff towards us. All is white. We can see only each other and the nearest ewes and rams.

Like that one on the ground asleep.

No, it's dead. Dried up and not all there.

Its friends don't seem perturbed. Indeed, it's not a morbid sight, but rather bucolic—sky, stones, grass, wool, bones. Eventually, we pass another fallen sheep here, another there. Not like a battlefield. More like, well, Nature: the living, the dead.

I feel of like mind with whomever has stewardship of these cliffs: why trudge down hauling the burden of each muddy carcass? Let the dead feed the . . . what? Vultures? Wolves? Insects? Feed the soil.

Such thoughts hold my interest for a bit, while we continue to put one foot in front of the other, up and up. Earlier in our travels, when we sought the Cooking Place, Bruce and I had that push-on /give-up dialogue. Now again, we alternate in our ambitions, but this time the interchange lasts for an *extended* infinity. We're sure we're approaching the peak, nothing but sky beyond that edge . . . only to find that the surrounding cloud conceals yet another slope. Oh, I should belt out a lament about how far and how high and how long we've hiked, far and away from all others of our species. I'll do the lyrics, and maybe Bruce will compose the music for "The Ballad of the *Farmisht* Travelers and the Sheep." (That's *ferMISHT*: Yiddish for confused, mixed-up, crazy.)

I think of *Brigadoon*, though yes, that's Scottish; maybe we'll find a magical occasional village. We have time, so I belt out, "Once in the highlands . . . two weary hunters lost their way . . .." Bruce suddenly lags behind, I'm sure to distance himself from the showtune. Undaunted, I proceed to, "When the mist is in the gloamin'/ and all the clouds are holding still/ if you're not here I won't go roamin'/ through the heather on the hill." Exhausting that production, I switch to "No he never returned/ and his fate is still unlearned/ Poor old Charlie/ He may ride forever/ 'neath the streets of Boston . . .."

Wait! I turn around to shout to Bruce "Look!" Stones, piled precisely on stones. The construction is rectangular, long as, oh let's see, four outhouses tipped and laid end-to-end. If it's meant to imitate a beehive, monks must not have studied insect architecture.

One opening. I hunch and go in. No windows.

Nearby, an identical structure. The sheep seem to have no use for them.

We try to conjure up a feeling of awe. "Neat." "Pretty old, huh?" "Guess they were something." We do convince ourselves that, by their shape, whatever these are, they are not beehive huts.

One of us wants to go on farther, thinking we *must* be near the real thing now. One of us says it's time to cash in our chips. As we carry on our lukewarm debate, our legs keep moving forward.

Eventually the moment comes when we agree to *cry uncle*. We're exhausted, yet we still have the wits to realize the sun will at sometime set, and sheep could go bump in the night. That structure we found would not make a cozy B&B. We both admit we couldn't care less about beehive huts.

Ireland*ish*   153

In My Backyard

From the sites of no beehives, we descend, down and down. How good it is to get back in our rental car and sit. Riding along, I catch sight of a postage-stamp-size sign: Ancient Beehive Huts

"Bruce, Bruce stop, there it is, there it was, we have to turn around."

Fools that we are, we do so.

A thatch-roofed cottage faces the road. We drive up the short bumpy dirt driveway and get out of the car; a weathered woman appears at the weathered door. She's pale-faced and no-color-haired, stout, in a limp, faded-yellow pinafore apron. I try to peek past her into the cottage; it's dark as a cave, save an unmistakable flickering glow. Peat fire? No: tv.

Hellos said, we ask how far away are the beehive huts.

"Sure they're right here. In my backyard."

Oy.

We tell her about our climb.

"Who told yeh the huts were up there?"

"Well, we looked at this map, and the woman at that restaurant . . .."

"Oh, that restaurant over there? They're new there, they are. Ten years I guess. I've never been way over to there."

We tell her of the long low stone structures we found.

"Ah, yeh *were* a ways up! Those would be the peat-drying houses."

Who traipses up into the clouds to cut chunks of earth, store them in shelters, and pack them down? Same people who finally invented the Presto log?

"My mother used to send us children up there to get peat

for our fires. They're not used anymore. Yeh *were* a ways up."

"So those weren't the beehive huts."

"Oh, no. Those are right here. In my backyard."

"Ah . . .. May we see them please?"

"Yes, sure," she says, holding out one hand, palm up. She informs us of how many *pence* to enter the huts, and how many *pence* to look at them from the outside.

Bruce says we'll stay outside, we just want to look around them. I say *I'll* be entering, thank you.

We hand her our separate fees, and she deftly tucks the money into her apron pocket. She directs us around to the back. Not ten yards away, amidst a grove of spreading trees and overgrown grasses, is a mounded stone structure.

I bend into its doorway. Not quite cozy; not quite awesome. Nicely piled rocks. I try to imagine sitting around *monking* in here all day. Nice hole in the ceiling. Nice dirt floor. Okay.

I exit and try another hut. Its personality has nothing to distinguish it from the first.

Well, then, that's that.

As we retreat towards our car, the woman appears at her doorway again, so we go over to thank her. Now her apron is gone; her t-shirt states, "I [heart] New York."

"Have you ever been to America?" I ask. I'm expecting her to say she's never traveled farther than fifty kilometers in her life, except for up.

What she does say: "Ah, sure, I've been to America seven times now. My grandchildren live there."

She adds, "But I can only go off-season."

"Off *what* season?"

"Off the tourist season. I have to be here when yeh come to see my huts."

I understand. Those pence from her backyard gold-mine must add up and transform into a pot of frequent-flier miles.

Maybe we should build a beehive hut tourist attraction in *our* backyard.

What We Miss

We don't visit all of the *must sees*. For one thing, we stay in the *Republic of* Ireland, skipping Northern Ireland altogether. At the beginning of our trip, the Aran Islands are but a ferry ride away; we decide we'll shop for woolens elsewhere. We don't check out caves, lighthouses, or boat tours. Not enamored of Irish step-dancing, we try to avoid touted shows of stick-figure clomping. I'm not sure why, but we don't visit any Montessori schools nor this country's teacher-training center of the international organization we're part of.

Soloists in folksong circles at home croon long, mournful Irish ballads, but we've encountered no balladeers here. Had we researched and planned better, it would have been fantastic for Bruce to immerse in the music of a big festival, a *caile* or *féile*. We don't see much green clothing; folks here don't seem to be *wearin' o'* it any more than do Philadelphians or Floridians when it's not March 17th. And, *hmm*, we haven't noticed even one real live shamrock. Guess we'll catch all that on our do-over.

Our Final Public House

We travel the still-wrong side of several roads back to Shannon for our last pubbing. Smoke, dark wooden furniture, laughter and gabbing and clinking glass, foam sliding down mugs, Guinness inhaled, Guinness exhaled. Once more Bruce plays; I tap my feet, sketch, eavesdrop, interview. From every corner, with or without an audience, the common woman and man expound on life's farce and tragedy. Nothing distinguishes this pub from the others.

I realize I'm feeling at home in this shared living room, where all seem included.

And now Bruce is soloing! Wow, he's become more confident. Not just any tune: it's his *own* "Green Eyes." Had I my druthers, he'd be gazing adoringly into my eyes right now, but of course he has to concentrate. As the other players pick up the tune and join in, and at the conclusion give grunts and nods of approval, my heart surges to see his cheek muscles rise slightly in that funny way, his endearing expression of a bit of embarrassment, a bit of humble pleasure.

Meanwhile, a smooth-faced man about my age, seated near me, is going on about how poor his family was when he was just a lad. "But *ah*, Mammy was a saint, she was, and brilliant with the purse strings, yeh know. She could feed the lot of us on sandwiches all made a'one egg."

The people near him nod, mumble, "Yeah, that's it"; "Ah, me blessed Mammy the same"; "To Mammy in heaven." They lift their pints in solidarity; I follow suit.

The first mammy-praiser fires up his voice and raises an open palm, to reclaim his pulpit. "And while the government looked away, and while the rich tried to pay their way through the pearly gates, wasn't she washing the clothes of the lot of us on her washboard!"

This elicits shouts: "Her fingers to the bone" and "The devils sure."

As he continues with, "But wasn't the Lord watching …," I'm wary of this sermon bombasting toward brimstone— until a crash of glass nearby brings on cheers all around, and the tormented preacher is abandoned, left alone with the moral of his memoir/harangue.

A Cool Farewell, or, I'm Scarlet

Our last home-away-from-home is a ladies' handiwork heaven, featuring all things pastel: lace curtains, cross-stitched cushions, doilies upon doilies, needlepointed bouquets. The lady of the house herself wears a pastel crocheted sweater and knit skirt, both of them stretched to their limits over her amply cushioned body.

Our final resting room smothers us in embroidered and appliqued pillows and duvets, spreads and comforters and bedskirts, topped by a yarn-y menagerie of kittens, giraffes, and unidentifiable critters.

After our ultimate emerald sleep, we rise early, eager to get past our Irish toast finale.

But first, my shower. "*AAAgghhh*! The water's *ice*."

I almost *plotz* while I grapple with the faucet handles. My efforts yield no satisfaction. Bruce reaches in to rescue me, but even he cannot force another degree of Celsius from this plumbing. Thankfully, there are towels. I dry, we dress and pack. We're opening the bedroom door, about to pull out our bags, when up the stairs trundles our hostess, crying, "Oh, there's no hot water in the house! Your shower, there's no hot water!" Mrs. Maloney or Delaney, or Mahoney is it? in any case *yer one*, has been a fine hostess who keeps the place embellished indeed. Now as she moans, "I'm so sorry, *oh dear*, what are we to do?" we insist, "Don't worry!" "It's fine." To no avail; she continues to keen as if it's her mother's funeral.

I try, "We've no need for showers this morning then, do we?"

We manage to convince her to come downstairs with us, murmuring assurances we've found her home to be splendid. I turn to see her lagging behind, wringing—actually wringing—her hands. At the bottom step, she scuttles off into the kitchen. As we sit at her table fingering the hand-woven placemats, we hear clatters and clacks, with an occasional shout, "Oh, I am coming I am," and "I'll make it up to yeh, I will!"

Eventually she carries in a tray laden with breakfast enough for the masses, including steaming porridge topped by the surprise of bananas (from the Irish tropics?) Plus, on the side, kiwis. A coffee pot, snug in a white felted cozy, and tea pot in its pink cozy. The pitcher of milk and its matching sugar bowl are naked of cozies yet replete with painted hydrangeas. Lovely eggs sit in shiny ceramic egg cups, and a molded wool basket covered by a scalloped cloth holds about seven more eggs for each of us. Out comes the dreaded so-called toast, in a rack, oh my, covered by a crocheted facsimile of a loaf of bread. Yes, we do find it hard to keep our faces straight.

She continues waddling back and forth, now bringing out yogurts of diverse flavors. A variety of dry cereals. Small cakes. "Ah, let's see, what else might yeh like? Sure yeh are yeh don't want bacon? Lovely bacon I have for yeh. Pancakes?"

We practically pull her down, onto a chair with a fuzzy braided throw over its back. What we really want: directions to get onto the *dual carriageway*—we know what that is!—to the airport. She gradually lets go of fretting enough to tell of her travels to Boston, and her daughter's employment with "the computer company." And yes those rose bushes outside are lovely, but it is not she who tends them, it's her hubby. "He's all the time feeding them this and that, and I swear the bushes are better nourished than me, not that yeh could tell by lookin' at me, mind yeh!"

She's had this business for twenty years. "When I first started there were only two with bed and breakfast establishments, myself and one other, in all of Shannon. But now will yeh look at them all!"

She returns to her "biggest concern this morning: the showers for yeh were cold!"

As I reach for and pat her hand, she continues, "Sure and it was the storm, that weather; the power was out last night, or was it two days ago when the rain was something awful? *Yer man* told me not to be using the kitchen when the guests might be showering upstairs."

Bruce told her that? I look pointedly at him. He too is startled. Oh, wait: she means her *hubby*.

She's going on, "So I never knew at all until too late that there was cold water only, and *agh!* I am *so so* sorry! I'm *scarlet* over it. I've given yeh some off on yer bill, a'course. No hot water, 'tis the worst *ting* that can happen in this business, the worst indeed!"

And finally she tells the directions.

The Last Word

At the airport we find one of those shopping-cart-type luggage carriers and pile on our stuff. We approach a gateway where the uniformed official scrutinizes our paperwork, hands it back, and announces, "Can't take the trolley!"

Fine, we're getting to a plane; we won't need a trolley. We step forward.

Now he's repeating loudly, "Can't take the trolley."

Okay, yeah. I push our stuff . . ..

The official's palm is now facing us in the *Stop* position and he's yelling, "CAN'T TAKE THE TROLLEY."

We both freeze.

I look to Bruce. Bruce looks to the man, then at our luggage.

Now Bruce says, "Oh. Jana, we *can't take the trolley.*"

I glare. "So. WHAT. Bruce."

He's heaving one of our bags over his shoulder, pulling another off the cart. I look at the guard and now notice the small turnstile behind him. Which this cart would never fit through. Aha, got it. Can't take the *trolley*.

The Non-Denouement of These Tales

The warp of this narrative should now weave into the weft, all matters explained and resolved.

Sorry, *luv*. At the end of the day, my conclusions about our trip to Ireland remain as mysterious as labyrinths, as puzzling as changelings. The spirals turn into each other; the knot has no end. Stories keep coming; they circle round to where they begin.

Life After

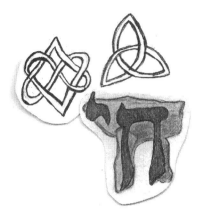

Only three days back on our own turf, we're barely, gratefully settling in. But hark, the Oregon Country Fair is about to come to life. Bruce, still full of spunk, is eager to travel the two hours for the unique event, an annual thrill. Jet lag and better judgment prompt me to skip it and stay home eating Bird's Custard and continuing to master Celtic knots. But Bruce puts aside his new Irish duds and puts on his batiked t-shirt and that "stupid hat," which he came by at last year's Fair. He's going.

Oh, wait, I don't want to miss out! So, soon we are together amidst thousands of lavish merrymakers.

This fair is not your 4H-goats-and-apple-pie gang. This is an earthy bubble of ecstatic artists and visionaries, passing around honey lemonade and massages, bongs, and bedazzling body paint. It features a literal tower of drum-beating. Art swirling from trees. Composting toilets and saunas and futuristic ideas. Good vibes tie-dyed onto banners and fried into delectable treats. A jingle-jangling tribal parade. (Stay with me in this crowd, please. This *is* relevant.) Something tells me we're not in Ireland anymore, yet not also in America, nor real life.

We've always favored the Fair's vaudeville acts: exotic, hilarious actors and musicians carousing through over-the-edge performances. But this too shall pass; now we whoop and applaud for the very last show and drop donations into the hat. I'm gathering my blanket and water bottle, snapping one more photo of partially clothed, fully rainbowed revelers, when, "Bruce? Where are you? Bruce?" I wriggle through the throng and find him yards away, leaning against a tree. He looks befuddled; he gasps he feels claustrophobic, his back's tight, his breath's short.

A blur of medics, gurney, ambulance, wires. We are sped to Eugene, the nearest city. Just outside the hospital emergency room, I clutch myself as I watch him get jolted by a defibrillator.

During his blessed recovery, Bruce recalls that back in Ireland just days before, on our ascent in pursuit of those dang beehive huts, he felt "a vague tightness" in his chest.

How differently things would have turned out, had what he calls his "heart event" progressed while the two of us were alone with the sheep, far far up in the Irish sky.

Cared for on our own turf, he survives. In fact, he becomes a poster child for after-heart-attack patients, partly because we stay away from our Cadburys and custard, cheeses of any origin, Guinness, and such.

By the By, or,
A Few Threads Followed

R*eturn to the Vernacular*   Though I intend to keep my new tongue oiled, that becomes tricky. For instance, the first time I am greeted at home with, "How are you?" I answer, "I'm lovely, thanks." The asker looks at me oddly. When I tell a waitress that mayonnaise on my sandwich would be *brilliant*, she averts her eyes. I find *grand* and *splendid* also just don't sit well here.

Within weeks, I drop those descriptors as well as my *luv* and *mammy*. My *lass, yer hubby,* and such *tings* slip away.

I fall reluctantly back into regular ol' U.S. talk, in which any and every feeling, experience, and sensation, if not "great," is "awesome," "good," "just fine," "very nice," or, most often, the *bland-iest*: "okay."

Okay then.

Undraped   Bruce's mother one evening complains she's freezing. I take my treasured Irish shawl from my shoulders and drape it over hers. She sighs and smiles in its caress. I leave it with her for the night.

And doesn't that splendid garment vanish into the maze of the assisted living facility?

Feckin' pity.

Remember the Waterford!   Our crystal golfing-prize vases from Maura and Alfie do make it, unscathed, all the way to our home shores. So do maybe two unnibbled Cadbury's. Maybe one.

But, just a few years later, where the heck have those vases gone? And why is Cadbury's here so bad?

The Potluck o' the Irish   Emails: "Catherine, how did it go when your mother hosted a potluck back in Ireland?"

"Ah, no. She never did get up the courage to ask her guests to bring the food! Never will."

Spiraling Back   The New Grange mysteries still turn and turn again within me. Looking into information and theories by astronomers, mathematicians, and other scientists, plus by fascinated laypeople, I've been been intrigued by the following:

If you were to mark on the ground the tip of the shadow of a tree or upright pole, every day for three moon cycles, your marks would define a spiral. And then in the next three months, they would define a second, connected spiral, and in the next three, another. One of these spirals would move in the opposite direction from the other two.

Let's test this out someday.

Solstice   I suspect I'll never know also how the so-called lottery is conducted at New Grange. At each winter solstice, I muse about the sun's early fingers lighting up that long entryway and those three sacred chambers, then leaving them again to pure blackness. I've yet to receive my invitation into those eleven minutes of wonder.

Good Riddance   Post-Ireland, there's occasional touch with Catherine. She used to give updates about Rory's increasingly troublesome shenanigans, his ongoing drinking and carousing. Some falsification about employment. Something about running off with a motorcyclist. As a family man, Rory was rather a *boyo* and a *slacker,* steadfast only in upholding an unfortunate stereotype. I found a relevant Irish saying: "Put a silk suit on a goat, it's still a goat." Bruce was always a loyal buddy, tending to amusement rather than judgment, but eventually he could no longer chuckle at the misbehavior of a *dosser.* Last heard, the lad took off over some dubious horizon. *May the road rise up to meet him,* as the famous Irish blessing goes. And, I add, may it knock some sense into his head.

Yet Another World   Nine years after our Irish adventure, Bruce and I have the opportunity to experience India. So different: not one redhead.

Swanny   We learn a plethora of theories and particulars about the owning, catching, and eating of swans. They include a medieval British declaration that all swans were the property of the monarch, so catching one (and being caught) would result in imprisonment in the Tower. *Select* non-royals were granted the privilege to mark a few swans for ownership by notching their beaks—*ouch*. Swans were eaten in Tudor times, and are even to this day by the occasional thieving connoisseur. But be warned: an angry swan can break a captor's legs with its wings. And a roasting swan, when the oven reaches a certain temperature, revives, and it haunts the cook.

All perhaps based on the rumor that swan meat is so delicious, the elite don't want commoners to partake.

Ah, the stories. Excellent deterrents. Not that I desire swanburgers anyway.

Deliciousness Past   Alas. Years later, when I wax lyrical to an acquaintance about Griffin's Bakery on Galway's Shop Street, she discovers it didn't make it long into this century. Sorry, luv, those crumbly, creamy, sticky delicacies have gone the way of the porridge that once filled the gigantic cauldron of plenty, gobbled by the hero Dagda. All now preserved only in legend.

And So

Our Irelandish tale was supposed to swirl around once again by the bays of sweet Glandore, where we would raise a glass in celebration of the fiftieth anniversary of our wedding. We looked forward to more of the trad *DI dilly DI,* lovely chocolate, hen parties, tall tales of the terrible and the grand, ancient stones, jokes at the Church's expense, donkey brays, freckled wee ones, leafy archways, cigarette smoke, warm Guinness, and Molly Malone.

As fate would have it, the body of my Bruce, survivor of a heart event, was invaded by the disease ALS. Six years before our anticipated return to Eire, he passed away.

Without him, I have not returned.

Yet that lovely, grand, splendid, and brilliant land, that myth, did manifest once for us, and I will always treasure its gift: these stories.

Appreciations

I so appreciate every person who helped create this adventure and its telling. Our brilliant Ooga Nooga Writing Group—Bob Sizoo, Elizabeth Stephenson, Kristina Bak, and Nancy Tyler, who make me kill several of my "darlings" and cool it on the em dashes. The splendid Judith Radovsky, who remains there/here for me; the grand Dawn Song who communicates compassion in every way; and my grand longtime long-distance gang, Jane McVeigh-Schultz, Maggie Smith, Mimsy Sadovsky, Paula Rubio, and Vickie Herzberg. They all listen and listen more. Catherine Callanan and the whole lot o' Irish folks, for being so very themselves. The knowledgeable women of Luminare Press. And all musicians, tellers, children, and the other *luvs*, past and present. Thank you!

Not a red hair was harmed in the making of this collection.

About the Author

Jana Zvibleman is the Poet Laureate of her backyard, now in Oregon. A storyteller by heredity, she has played with other poets as well as sculptors, journalists, painters, theater-types, buskers, and a flugelhornist. She is also a photographer, essayist, artist-on-the-loose, plus teacher of writing and other life-saving techniques. Her books and chapbooks include *Bruyote Tales*; *The Old Woman Next Door and the Next Old Woman's Door*; and *The Bad Mothers*.

Her name is pronounced: J (as in J) ana (rhymes with bandana) ZWEE bel mn (not really that hard)

Made in United States
Troutdale, OR
10/07/2024

23486611R00104